Praise for Machine Learning – Getting Started

"Great source to begin your machine learning journey to understand the fundamentals of machine learning, deep learning, and natural language processing techniques. This book provides easy-to-understand concepts and will serve as a jump start to advance to the next level. There are actionable steps to take your knowledge to the industry."

— Himanshu Parikh, Senior Vice President,
Global Chief Information Officer, Footlocker

"This book is for inquisitive beginners who want to cut through the buzz words and build their first machine learning model while reading. If you want to get exposure to machine learning, this book addresses the fundamentals to get you grounded. It outlines the machine learning subject in simple English, with the right amount of foundations."

— Mehul Doshi, Chief Product &
Technology Officer, ACT

"The book is a good resource for someone starting new and excited to get exposed to machine learning. It covers many theoretical concepts while showcasing its practical application using python. It includes topics that cover necessary mathematical foundations like calculus and statistics, which are not common in similar books. Well-written and easy-to-follow through the structure from start to finish."

— Pavan Baruri, Global Head of Digital Engineering,
BISSELL Homecare Inc.,

**Machine Learning – Getting Started © Copyright 2022
Ananda Soundhararajan**

For more information, email asoundhararajan@gmail.com
Visit www.letsbecomemlengineers.com

ISBN: 9798840630822

Machine Learning - Getting Started

Launch yourself into machine learning!

Let's Become
ML Engineers

Ananda Soundhararajan

Dedication

Idedicate this book to my dad (my superhero), the best leader I have ever seen in my life.

I am grateful to my wife Nisha and my two daughters - Anvita and Akshita; they sacrificed a lot when I spent late-nights on this book. I am eternally grateful to my mom, and my high school mentor Mr.Gnanasekharan for encouraging me to pursue my passion for computer science engineering.

Thank you Praveen Kadala, for making my machine learning journey smoother, and I appreciate every minute of your time and valuable inputs from you to bring this book out the door.

It is my first book; I am grateful to the following people for helping me become a better person every single day.

I acknowledge Dr. Shiv Nadar, philanthropist, and founder of HCL Technologies, SSN College of Engineering, for his generous contribution to the people who need financial assistance and enabling students like me to focus solely on their dreams.

My leadership coach - Vamsi Polimetla, Make More Leaders

My Board of Directors - Venkat Hari, Manoharan Sridharan, Srinivas Yarlagadda, Devakumar Sai Chinthala, Bharat Ramesh and Mugunthu Dhananjeyan

My loveable content and copy editors - Uzal Chhetri, Bianca-Adina Szasz, Sujata Supanekar and Sowmya Thanigachalam.

My creative team who designed the fantastic book cover and outline images- Swathi Atloori, Nisha Anand and Ravi Ramgati

My favorite Lake County Toastmasters and the D30 Toastmasters, the best team you could get on your side!

Finally, all the medical professionals who helped us to get through COVID by sacrificing their family time.

Table of Contents

Chapter 7 : Deep Learning ... 101

**Chapter 10 : The Machine
Learning Engineer ... 151**

Live as if you were to die tomorrow.

Learn as if you were to live forever.

— Mahatma Gandhi

CHAPTER 1

Introduction

What & Why

One of my favorite quotes on short-term and long-term solutions is, "give a man a fish and you feed him for a day; teach a man to fish and you feed him for a lifetime." This saying applies to many things in life, including machine learning. You can compare "giving a man a fish" to traditional computer programming where you solve an immediate problem, but machine learning is the "teach a man how to fish" part of the statement. Teaching the computer not just to solve the immediate problem at hand and also the similar problems you will encounter in the future. While traditional computer programming provides us with instant solutions, the benefits of machine learning can be reaped over the years.

We are living in the most defining period of human history. In this era, computing has moved from large mainframe PCs to the cloud. What makes this period significant is not the events leading up to this moment, but what is going to happen from hereon. A future created by machine learning and data.

1.1 ARTIFICIAL INTELLIGENCE

Machine learning is a sub-category of artificial intelligence (AI). The term "Artificial Intelligence" was coined by John McCarthy, a computer scientist.

Artificial intelligence is the science and engineering of making intelligent machines, especially intelligent computer programs. AI is not what the movies make it out to be. You can imagine AI as a computer program that is able to mimic some of the human brain's cognitive abilities. Cognitive abilities like learning, thinking, reasoning, and decision making. Now, the human mind is capable of many things of varied complexities. You can code a simple decision a human mind can make but you cannot code how the mind thinks about abstract things. To make things easier, AI has been categorized into two different types:

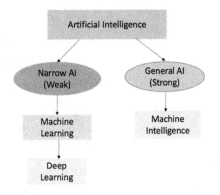

Figure 1: *Artificial Intelligence types.*

1.1.1 Narrow AI

Narrow AI is the type of AI that is very good at doing a particular task, and nothing more than that. If you look at AI for playing chess, it is very good at playing chess but it would be worse than useless in identifying images. It is like a person who trained his whole life perfecting the art of doing something that he completely forgot how to live and be a normal human being.

Most AI systems that you know most probably are narrow AI implementations. Systems like Google Assistant, Google Translate, Siri, and Amazon Alexa are all examples of narrow AI.

A narrow AI also lacks self-awareness, consciousness, and genuine intelligence to match human intelligence, making it unable to think for itself.

1.1.2 General AI

Also called strong AI, general AI refers to hypothetical AI systems that have intelligence comparable to human beings. These systems will be able to perform intellectual tasks just like you. This type of AI has still not been designed in real-life and there are many researchers trying to make it a reality. A fictional example of this type of AI can be Data in the Star Trek movies.

1.2 MACHINE LEARNING

Arthur Lee Samuel (a pioneer in artificial intelligence) defines machine learning as a "field of study that gives computers the ability to learn without being explicitly programmed."

Machine learning in itself is a very vast field, and areas such as deep learning (DL) are sub-fields of machine learning.

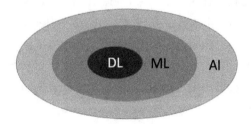

Figure 2: *Venn Diagram Showing the Fields of Artificial Intelligence.*

Machine learning has been around since the 1960s, but it has received mainstream attention only in recent years. What has changed that made it possible for machine learning to be adopted by the masses?

Well, one thing is that the true capability of machine learning had been held behind by the lackluster hardware for many years. In the recent years, there has been a huge advancement in computational power, most of it owing to the improvements seen in GPUs (Graphical Processing Units). Yes, the same GPU that runs your games has the capability to run deep learning algorithms. Not only have there been improvements in GPUs, but also there are numerous cheap cloud solutions now available to access these powerful GPUs by even small companies and hobbyists wanting to learn more.

Machine learning also requires massive amount of data to train its models for it to start predicting in real-time. We have seen growing interest in Internet of Things (IoT) devices in recent years. Each and every one of these devices is a way to collect data, and this data can be processed and used to make models perform better.

Due to the two factors mentioned above, there has been a lot of breakthroughs in machine learning and deep learning research. Research has also been conducted in backpropagation algorithms, and new neural network models that perform better than the previous ones have been introduced.

As a result of these advances, machine learning has reached the forefront of the artificial intelligence discipline, but AI has much broader applications than machine learning alone. Andrew Ng, a computer scientist, quoted, "AI is the new electricity. It will transform every industry and create huge economic value." After you read this book, it will be hard not to agree with him. From this book, you will also comprehend the importance of AI, and the fact that it will have an impact in every sector – everything including healthcare to manufacturing, logistics, and retail.

1.2.1 Machine Learning vs. Automation

A lot of the machine learning tasks seem like automation to people who have not been initiated into the world of machine learning. When you look at it, what is Google Translate other than an automated way of translating without using human translators? But there is a world of difference between automation and machine learning models.

Automation is usually doing something repetitively following a set of rules. This is called rule-driven automation. In contrast, machine learning is where a system learns from past data and makes decisions regarding the new data. A machine learning model has the ability to learn something new when new data comes in, and it can always be updated without hardcoding a rule.

You can think of automation as a robot in a factory tasked to carry a car chassis from one level to another. This robot is programmed specifically to perform the same task in a loop. In that same factory, there might be another robot that looks at the car parts and finds the defective ones and throws them out. This robot is one with sensors and a computer vision model that cannot be hard coded like the first robot.

Automation is an example of traditional programming where data and a program are run on a computer to produce an output. Whereas, machine learning has the data and output run on a computer to create a program.

Figure 3: *Difference between the Traditional Approach to Programming and the Machine Learning Model*

1.2.2 Why Choose Machine Learning over Traditional Programming?

There are many applications where traditional programming is better suited than machine learning but in cases of spam filtering, handwriting recognition, autonomous driving amongst many other applications, machine learning is preferred.

One simple criterion for choosing between machine learning and traditional programming is to ask yourself this simple question, "will the input to my system be the same every single time?" If the answer to that question is yes, then you do not need machine learning for that specific use case. If in your use case the input changes (maybe you have to create a Chatbot using data from a chatroom where people are free to express themselves in any way possible), then a machine learning algorithm will perform better.

Let's take the example of a Chatbot, to use traditional programming methods to create one would be close to impossible. The task of data mining (FYI, data mining is the process of finding patterns in data, not going around collecting data or web-scraping to get data) using traditional programming method needs to encompass all the different ways and methods humans may express themselves to the Chatbot. Keeping track of all the small rules in written human conversations is difficult enough (as a human being!), imagine doing that by writing lines after lines of code.

Suppose we assume that you are a maestro of human communication, and you know all the rules of written human communication. Even in this case, writing the software will be a bottleneck and you could never be able to write all the lines of code required.

An easier alternative would be to use machine learning algorithms to model the written human communication. You only need a handful of code to create an algorithm that understands basic written communication. Machine learning will then automatically perform human communication tasks by self-learning through a lot of trial and error. You can also feed this model with new data so that your model never stops learning and growing.

1.2.3 Why Should I Learn Machine Learning?

Mark Cuban put it best, "artificial intelligence, deep learning, machine learning – whatever you're doing, if you don't understand it – learn it. Because otherwise you're going to be a dinosaur within 3 years."

I agree with Mark Cuban, and even programming skills are vulnerable to being automated thereby reducing the number of programming jobs.

Almost all companies, in all different sectors are trying to integrate machine learning into their functions. This will lead to a lot of new opportunities for aspiring machine learning engineers. Even today, there is a huge gap between what the industry needs and what is on the table right now.

To list a few achievements of machine learning:

- OpenAI's bot won DotA 2 matches over the world's best teams in this game. For those who don't know, DotA 2 is a strategy game where you need to have teamwork and fast reflexes as well as good planning and strategies to win
- Google DeepMind's algorithm beat Lee Sidol at the traditional game of GO.
- OpenAI's GPT-2 can write entire essays, poetry as well as create movies from scratch using NLP techniques.
- Creating and generating images and videos from scratch (this is both incredibly creative and worryingly accurate)
- Google created TensorFlow.js that allows for the building of machine learning models in the browser itself

Now let's look into what machine learning really is, and go over some technical details.

1.3 AN OVERVIEW OF MACHINE LEARNING

Machine learning can be categorized into the following criteria:

1. Amount of supervision
2. Learning approach
3. Learning mode

Let us see these categories in more detail:

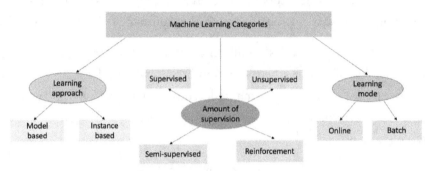

Figure 4: *Machine Learning categories*

1.3.1 Amount of Supervision

Supervised Learning

In supervised learning, there will be an input and a corresponding output. So, all you have to do is to find a mapping function from the input to the output. Classification and regression are typical supervised learning tasks.

For example, when you are training an e-mail spam filter, you will have an e-mail and its actual output and whether that e-mail is spam or not. The model that you create will make a lot of mistakes but eventually learn what type of e-mails are spam and the ones that are not.

Some examples of supervised learning algorithms are linear regression, logistic regression, k-nearest neighbors, support vector machines, decision trees and random forests, and neural networks (this can be unsupervised too).

Unsupervised Learning

In unsupervised learning, the data is not labelled. You can say that it only has an input without a set output unlike in supervised learning. You will need to find patterns and functions that describe the data really well to get anything meaningful out of the dataset.

An example of this type of learning will be what retail corporations currently do. They take all the data available to them and group customers into frequent and infrequent visitors to target promotions to individuals. In this case, the retailers only have the information about when you bought something from their outlet, and they take this data and find the frequency of visits and the different products you buy each time. In other words, they take simple data and find patterns in the data and compare it with the data they have on other customers.

Some unsupervised learning algorithms include k-means clustering, anomaly detection, and dimensionality reduction.

Semi-Supervised Learning

This learning type is most commonly seen in the real world. In this case, the data will be partially labelled, and you need to use the partially labelled data to your advantage to train a model that eventually works with unlabeled data.

For example, the text document classifier is a common application of semi-supervised learning.

Most semi-supervised algorithms are a combination of supervised and unsupervised algorithms. For example, deep belief networks (DBNs) stack restricted Boltzmann machine as its building blocks. DBNs can be used in both unsupervised settings for tasks such as image generation and in supervised settings for tasks such as image classification.

Reinforcement Learning

This type of learning is inspired from human psychological behavior, where there is an agent inside an environment. This agent performs actions inside the environment to get rewards or penalties based on positive or negative outcomes of the action it performed. The agent likes to get rewards and dislikes penalties, so it is trained to get the most rewards over time.

DeepMind's AlphaGo program is the most popular example of reinforcement learning. It beat the world champion of the Go game,

Ke Jie, at the game and this achievement was all over the news in May 2017.

Some common reinforcement learning algorithms are q-learning, temporal difference, and deep adversarial networks.

1.3.2 Batch Learning vs. Online Learning

Batch Learning is also called offline learning. In this type of learning, you train the data using all the available data. If you want this model to learn new data, you need to train the new version of the system from scratch using the full dataset, replacing the old system.

Online learning is the type of learning where the model trains in real-time. It keeps learning as new data comes in while making real-time predictions. The problem with this type of learning is that if bad data comes into the system, prediction accuracy declines gradually which will impact the live consumers of the system. You will need to monitor the incoming data to detect anomalies to avoid bad customer experience.

1.3.3 Instance-based Learning vs. Model-based Learning

Instance-based learning algorithms use the entire dataset as a model. It learns the training examples by heart and generalize it to the new instances based on the similarity measure. It is called instance-based learning as it builds the hypothesis based on training instances. There is no model to persist here, but we will need to retain the training datasets for future learnings. Storing the entire training dataset may incur additional storage costs.

One popular example of instance-based learning is k-nearest neighbor (KNN). KNN finds the similarity of new data to the pre-existing data already modeled. It can recommend similar products to users using this method.

Model-based learning uses the training data to create a model that has parameters learnt from the training data. Prediction for new instances is faster compared to instance-based learning. Once the model is built, we can discard the training data and store just the model to save storage costs.

Neural networks are a popular example of model-based learning. Other examples might include support vector machine (SVM), and random forest.

1.4 MACHINE LEARNING LIFE CYCLE

The algorithm trained on a data becomes a model. Usually, the first model you train is not going to be a good one. You need to fine-tune the model to make it perform better. Here is a tip when designing models: Your model is only as good as your data.

The figure below shows the basic steps of creating a machine learning model:

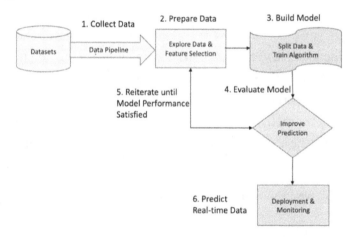

Figure 5: *Steps Involved in Deploying a Machine Learning Model*

Let us imagine that you want to build a machine learning model that recognizes handwritten alphabets and numbers. The first thing you need to do is collect as much relevant data as you can. There needs to be a minimum of 1000 different examples per class. In this case, you want at least a 1000 different handwritten 'a's, 'b's, 'c's and so on.

Once you have all the data, you need to explore the data and find patterns in your data. Maybe your data has 5000 'a's but only 1000 '1's. This is called an imbalance in class. In machine learning, it is always better to have equal number of datapoints per class. In this step, you will delete all the unwanted data points, balance the classes, and also normalize the dataset so that each data point is comparable with the other data points. An example of normalizing is converting all handwritten images into pixels in the range of 0 – 1.

After you explore the dataset and select the required features, you need to split the dataset. This is done because you want an unbiased performance report of the model. If you train the model and then test the model with the same datasets, it will always perform better in training and testing, but its real-time predictions will be poor. The dataset is usually divided into 3 sets called train, test, and validation. You can pick how to divide the dataset, but the train dataset usually has 80% of the total data, with test and validation having 10% data each.

Next, you need to pick the algorithm that you will be using to classify the dataset. You can pick a convolutional neural network to classify the handwritten dataset. After training the model, you need to evaluate it using the test dataset. If the performance of the model does not satisfy you, then you need to go back and fine-tune the model and perform the whole feature selection, splitting and training of the model again. You will do this until you are happy with the outcome.

Finally, when you are satisfied with your model, you can deploy it.

1.5 WHAT YOU WILL LEARN IN THIS BOOK

I love the machine learning courses from Coursera, Udacity, or Udemy, but those are more of an academic style. If you take those courses (you might have taken one before), the subject seems dry and math-heavy with formulae and derivative equations. But machine learning is not dry and uninteresting, there are a lot of different applications of machine learning that are very engaging. If you want to deploy models, you can deploy them by understanding the high-level concepts. If you have an intuitive understanding of how the models work, you can plug-and-play with the models.

There are excellent libraries to abstract the statistical models (scikit-learn), and frameworks for deep learning models (TensorFlow, Keras, PyTorch) out there. They are all easy to learn if you have a few years of software development experience.

You just need to brush up on a little bit of your high school linear algebra, calculus, probability and statistical concepts. There is no pre-requisite to have a Master's or PhD degree in data science to become a good machine learning engineer.

There are so many machine learning algorithms that you might feel overwhelmed when people throw them at you, but once you get a high-level understanding of the machine learning concepts, you can deep dive based on the type of problem you want to solve. It is all about taking the first baby step which seems hard and daunting as there are too many new terminologies to absorb. Once you get your hands wet with a "hello world" machine learning model, everything else will fall in place.

In this book, my goal is to get you up to speed with a high-level understanding of machine learning so that you hit the ground running in about 10 weeks. There will be a git source code repo folder for each chapter with Jupyter notebooks to get your hands dirty and understand the concepts better.

My vision for this book is to create interest and excitement about the machine learning field and simplify your machine learning journey as much as possible.

I have included all the sources I refer to in the book in the References section. I am still learning, and I hope you will also be a lifelong learner of machine learning given the depth and the continuous breakthroughs in deep learning.

1.6 SUMMARY

- AI is a broad term for creating and designing intelligent machines.

- Most of the current AIs in the market are what are known as Narrow AI.

- Machine learning is a sub-field of AI, and deep learning is a sub-field of machine learning.

- There is a difference between traditional programming and machine learning because a machine learning model trains itself and continuously improves without human intervention while the traditional applications do not.

- If you have a problem where the input data keeps on changing due to human actions or just nature, then you need a machine learning algorithm to solve that problem for you.

- A machine learning algorithm can be supervised, unsupervised, semi-supervised, or reinforced. It can be instance-based or model-based. It can be online, or batch-learnt.

- You do not need to be a math prodigy to learn how a machine learning algorithm works, and this book will show you just how.

Now that you have reached the end of the first chapter, you should go ahead to https://github.com/a-soundhararajan/machine-learning/tree/main/HelloWorld to build your first 'hello world' machine learning model.

Please refer to the readme.MD page to setup your machine learning workspace. I am assuming you are familiar with the Python programming language. If not, no big deal, you can get up to speed in Python in a week easily.

There is additional content on my website https://letsbecomemlengineers.com/ and YouTube channel (https://www.youtube.com/channel/UcxxGU_Q6A-8aJlSGP19FYUA), I highly recommend that you check it out.

CHAPTER 2

Data

It's All About Data

Data is the new oil of the digital economy, fueling the fourth industrial revolution. With data growing exponentially over the last few years, AI has also advanced by leaps and bounds. Bigger and better machine learning models are coming out every day, achieving tremendous results in image processing, computer vision, and natural language processing.

2.1 DATA

As of 2020, worldwide data generation reached 44 zettabytes. Interestingly, according to www.seedscientific.com, 90% of all data ever generated was in the last five years. By 2025, we are expected to hit 463 exabytes of data creation and 75 billion Internet of Things (IoT) devices globally.

Google handles a staggering 1.2 trillion searches every year. Now imagine the amount of data the search algorithms have to navigate through to get you relevant results in a fraction of a second. Given the anticipated data growth in the upcoming years, the traditional rule-based or heuristic approach fails to meet the new demands.

You might be thinking, why should we care about data so much? To create a good machine learning model, you need equally massive and high-quality data to feed into the model. You could say that when it comes to machine learning algorithms, it heavily relies on the kind of data you feed. "Garbage in, Garbage out." Your machine model accuracy is as good as the data (dish) you feed in for training, similar to "you are what you eat."

Let's say that you have the raw to build a machine learning model. We will now talk about transforming the raw data into features that can produce a good machine learning model. There are usually two steps to this:

1. Exploratory Data Analysis
2. Feature Engineering

2.2 EXPLORATORY DATA ANALYSIS

Exploratory data analysis (EDA) refers to the process of performing initial investigations on data to discover patterns, identify anomalies, test hypotheses, and check assumptions with the help of statistics and visual representations. Data contains many underlying trends. By understanding these trends, data engineers can learn more about the data and its features.

According to John Tukey (mathematician and statistician, who developed the box plot algorithm), "exploratory data analysis is an attitude, a state of flexibility, a willingness to look for those things that we believe are not there, as well as those we believe to be there."

To understand EDA in detail, let us explore the Titanic dataset as a learning example. You can download the Titanic dataset from Kaggle (https://www.kaggle.com/c/titanic/data).

2.2.1 Titanic Dataset Details

Variable	Description	Key/Value
survived	This is the label of whether the person survived.	0 = No 1 = Yes
Pclass	Ticket Class 1st: Upper Class 2nd: Middle Class 3rd: Lower Class	6 = 2st 2 = 2nd 3 = 3rd
sex	Gender	male/female
age	Age in years	
SibSp	Number of siblings/spouses aboard the Titanic Sibling: brother, sister, stepbrother, stepsister Spouse: husband, wife (mistresses and fiancés were ignored).	
parch	Number of parents/children aboard the Titanic Parent: mother, father Child: daughter, son, stepdaughter, stepson Some children travelled only with a nanny, therefore, parch=0 for them.	
ticket	Ticket number	
fare	Passenger fare	
cabin	Cabin number	
embarked	Port of embarkation	C: Cherbourg Q: Queenstown S: Southampton

2.2.2 Data Manipulation and Analysis using Pandas

Python's pandas library allows us to read data in many formats such as CSV, Excel, and SQL. There are many functions that make exploring your data so much easier. We will look at some of them in this section

- "dataset.head()" and "dataset.tail()" functions return the first 5 observations and the last 5 observations of the dataset, respectively.

```
In [2]: import pandas as pd
        train=pd.read_csv("train.csv")
        train.head()
```

Out[2]:

	PassengerId	Survived	Pclass	Name	Sex	Age	SibSp	Parch	Ticket	Fare	Cabin	Embarked
0	1	0	3	Braund, Mr. Owen Harris	male	22.0	1	0	A/5 21171	7.2500	NaN	S
1	2	1	1	Cumings, Mrs. John Bradley (Florence Briggs Th...	female	38.0	1	0	PC 17599	71.2833	C85	C
2	3	1	3	Heikkinen, Miss. Laina	female	26.0	0	0	STON/O2. 3101282	7.9250	NaN	S
3	4	1	1	Futrelle, Mrs. Jacques Heath (Lily May Peel)	female	35.0	1	0	113803	53.1000	C123	S
4	5	0	3	Allen, Mr. William Henry	male	35.0	0	0	373450	8.0500	NaN	S

Figure 1: *Pandas head() Function*

- You can check the total number of rows and columns in the dataset using the function "dataset.shape".

```
In [3]: train.shape
Out[3]: (891, 12)
```

Figure 2: *Pandas dataset.shape Attribute*

- The "dataset.info()" function displays columns and their datatypes, along with finding whether they contain null values or not.

```
In [4]: train.info()
<class 'pandas.core.frame.DataFrame'>
RangeIndex: 891 entries, 0 to 890
Data columns (total 12 columns):
 #   Column       Non-Null Count  Dtype
---  ------       --------------  -----
 0   PassengerId  891 non-null    int64
 1   Survived     891 non-null    int64
 2   Pclass       891 non-null    int64
 3   Name         891 non-null    object
 4   Sex          891 non-null    object
 5   Age          714 non-null    float64
 6   SibSp        891 non-null    int64
 7   Parch        891 non-null    int64
 8   Ticket       891 non-null    object
 9   Fare         891 non-null    float64
 10  Cabin        204 non-null    object
 11  Embarked     889 non-null    object
dtypes: float64(2), int64(5), object(5)
memory usage: 83.7+ KB
```

Figure 3: *Pandas dataset.info() Method*

- The "dataset.describe()" method summarizes the data columns statistically. It analyzes all data types, including numeric, object, and mixed data but generally works better for numeric data types. It returns the statistical summary of the data columns in the form of mean, standard deviation, minimum value, maximum value, count, and three percentiles (25%, 50%, and 75%).

```
In [5]: train.describe()
Out[5]:
```

	PassengerId	Survived	Pclass	Age	SibSp	Parch	Fare
count	891.000000	891.000000	891.000000	714.000000	891.000000	891.000000	891.000000
mean	446.000000	0.383838	2.308642	29.699118	0.523008	0.381594	32.204208
std	257.353842	0.486592	0.836071	14.526497	1.102743	0.806057	49.693429
min	1.000000	0.000000	1.000000	0.420000	0.000000	0.000000	0.000000
25%	223.500000	0.000000	2.000000	20.125000	0.000000	0.000000	7.910400
50%	446.000000	0.000000	3.000000	28.000000	0.000000	0.000000	14.454200
75%	668.500000	1.000000	3.000000	38.000000	1.000000	0.000000	31.000000
max	891.000000	1.000000	3.000000	80.000000	8.000000	6.000000	512.329200

Figure 4: *Pandas dataset.describe() Method*

There are a lot more functions that you can use to get an insight into the dataset that you are working with. To give you a few examples, we did the following to get a feeling of the "Survived" variable of our dataset.

```
In [7]: train.Survived.unique()
Out[7]: array([0, 1])

In [8]: train.Survived.value_counts()
Out[8]: 0    549
        1    342
Name: Survived, dtype: int64
```

Figure 5: *Exploring the "Survived" Column of the Dataset*

2.2.3 Data Visualization with Matplotlib and Seaborn

You now know how to read data and explore the data, but an image speaks a thousand words, so there must be a better way to explore the dataset than reading the output from a table. That's where matplotlib and seaborn comes in.

Both libraries allow you to visualize the data that you throw at them. Seaborn is built on top of matplotlib, so you can pick whatever you wish to use. For now, we will discuss seaborn and the different visualization options it provides.

Heatmaps

Heatmaps are used to visualize correlations. Correlation refers to the statistical relationship between two variables, either positive or negative. A positive correlation exists if the value of both variables increases or decreases in the same direction, and a negative correlation exists if the value of one variable increases while the other decreases.

It is necessary to remove correlated variables to improve your machine learning model. We can find correlations using pandas "corr()" function and can visualize the correlation matrix using seaborn's "heatmap()" function.

The "heatmap()" function has an "annot" attribute. If you set annot=True, you'll get values by which features are correlated to each other in grid-cells. Dark shades represent positive correlation, while lighter shades represent negative correlation. Here you can see that the dependent variable "Survived" has a positive correlation with "Fare" and negative correlation with "Pclass".

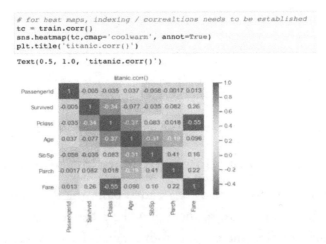

Figure 6: Heatmap

Generally, if two independent variables are highly correlated, either positively or negatively, we can safely drop one of them as both represent similar data trends. Usually, the model would not benefit from learning closely related features. If the correlation is zero, we can infer that there is no linear relationship between these two features.

If you are building a machine learning model like linear regression, variables without any linear relationship can adversely affect the model's performance. In such a case, we can safely drop all features that have zero correlation to improve the model output.

Box Plot

Also known as the box-and-whisker plot, seaborn's box plot displays the data distribution of variables for quantitative comparison. It can compare the categorical levels within a variable. The box plot is commonly used to display and identify outliers in a variable using the interquartile range (IQR) function. The box (rectangle) in the box plot represents the data quartiles (first quartile to the third quartile), while the whiskers represent the remaining data distribution.

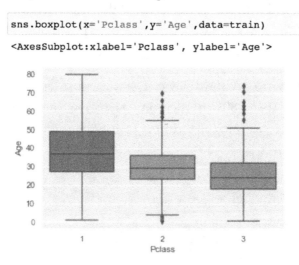

```
sns.boxplot(x='Pclass',y='Age',data=train)

<AxesSubplot:xlabel='Pclass', ylabel='Age'>
```

Figure 7: *Seaborn Box Plot*

Most of the time, people tend to overlook or skip the EDA step, but this is one of the most important steps in producing the best model one can. It shows whether your data is linearly distributed or if there is a non-linear distribution. EDA provides valuable insights in to deciding which model works best for your dataset. Performing EDA works like the the Pareto principle (80/20 rule). It is the 20% effort required to get 80% value in terms of choosing the correct model and achieving better prediction accuracy.

2.3 FEATURE ENGINEERING

Feature engineering is the process of extracting important features from raw data and transforming them into formats that machine learning models can understand and learn. It requires expert domain knowledge to extract valuable features from the existing data. High-quality data features directly affect the machine learning model's performance. Feature engineering gives more flexibility to the data scientist because good features can work well with almost any kind of machine learning model.

Feature engineering has two main goals:

1. Extracting high-quality features from the input dataset that are aligned with the requirements of the machine learning algorithm.

2. Improving the predictive capabilities of the machine learning models until the desired performance is achieved.

According to a CrowdFlower Data Science Report (2016) survey, data scientists spend 80% of their time preparing data before considering which machine learning algorithms to use for training:

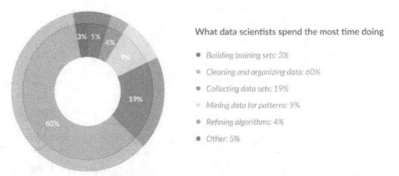

Figure 8: *CrowdFlower Data Science Report, 2016 (GilPress, 2016)*

Feature engineering is an art as well as a science. It is an iterative trial-and-error process, which is the reason why data scientists spend majority of their time in the data preparation phase before they even begin modeling. Experts in the field reiterate its importance as below:

"Coming up with features is difficult, time-consuming, requires expert knowledge. 'Applied machine learning' is basically feature engineering."

— *Prof. Andrew Ng, Stanford University,*
co-founder of Coursera

"Feature engineering is the process of transforming raw data into features that better represent the underlying problem to the predictive models, resulting in improved model accuracy on unseen data."

— *Dr. Jason Brownlee,*
founder of www.machinelearningmasttery.com

"At the end of the day, some machine learning projects succeed, and some fail. What makes the difference? Easily the most important factor is the features used."

— *Prof. Pedro Domingos,*
University of Washington

2.3.1 Problems with Data

When you work with real-world data, you will run into several problems like insufficient data, too much data, non-representative data, missing data, and duplicate data. That's where feature engineering techniques come to the rescue. These data problems are discussed in detail in the Training chapter (# 3).

2.3.2 Data Preparation Stage

Data preparation is the foundation of building robust machine learning pipelines that achieve better prediction accuracy. Data preparation is a multi-stage process that consists of data preprocessing, data wrangling, feature extraction, feature scaling, and feature selection. A typical data pipeline is given below:

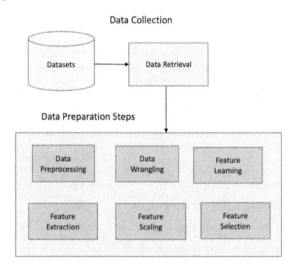

Figure 9: *Data Pipeline*

Raw data is generally located in a database or a data warehouse. You'll need to set up pipelines to extract the data from where it is stored, then clean and prepare the data for modeling.

Real-world data cannot be used directly to train machine learning models. It needs to be processed. We need to get rid of missing values and remove outliers. If you have non-numeric representations of data, they must be encoded in the numeric form. Data preparation is difficult and time-consuming, and all of these steps encompass feature engineering.

2.3.3 No One Size Fits All

Feature engineering is specific to the problem domain. There is no common set of techniques that apply to all classifiers or regressors. You can't say that one kind of feature engineering works best for neural networks, whereas another kind works best for traditional statistical models. It's an engineering where you bring features together in a form that helps to build robust models. There is no one size fits all.

2.3.4 Scope of Feature Engineering

Feature engineering is a broad umbrella that encompasses the methods mentioned below:

1. **Feature Selection:** Choosing the best subset from an existing set of features without transforming or changing the features in any manner. Let's say you have many X-variables present in your data. During exploratory data analysis, you've found that only a few X-variables are very meaningful and have high predictive power, and further these meaningful variables are independent of each other. You will then use feature selection to choose only those meaningful variables to train your model.

2. **Feature Learning:** Due to real-world data complexity, feature selection cannot scale if it only relies on humans. This is where feature learning or representation learning comes into the picture, the model has to learn to identify important features from complex data like images and videos. Traditional ML systems rely on human experts to decide which features are important. Representation-based ML systems figure out important features by themselves. Neural networks are examples of representation-based ML systems.

3. **Feature Extraction:** Feature extraction differs from feature selection. In feature extraction, input features are fundamentally transformed into derived features. The derived features are often unrecognizable and hard to interpret. These derived features represent numerical patterns present in the original features.

4. **Feature Combination:** This involves aggregating independent features to curate a feature with more predictive power. Let's say we are predicting the traffic pattern of a city. You might get traffic information for a day of the week and a specific time of that day. When the day of the week and the time of the day are aggregated, you can find the resulting feature that has more predictive power. For example, traffic on Friday 6:00

PM will be more accurately predicted and totally different from that on another day at a specific time, like Sunday 6:00 PM.

5. **Dimensionality Reduction:** When you're working with real-world data, managing large datasets is quite challenging. Having datasets with hundreds of complex features is a curse and is often referred to as the curse of dimensionality. When you work with high dimensionality datasets, data visualization becomes challenging, and machine learning models find it hard to identify patterns leading to poor quality overfitted models. Dimensionality reduction is a form of unsupervised learning that explicitly aims to solve the curse of dimensionality while preserving as much of the original information as possible from the underlying features.

2.3.5 Feature Engineering Techniques

Some feature engineering techniques work better with only some algorithms or datasets, while others may work in all cases. Following are some of the most commonly used feature engineering techniques applicable on real-world datasets.

Imputation

Feature engineering usually begins by identifying the missing values in the input dataset. Datasets might have missing values due to unintended human errors, interruptions in the data flow, privacy concerns, and so on. Missing values affect the performance of the machine learning models. The simplest solution is to drop the rows or the entire columns that contain missing values. However, imputation is a preferable option over dropping because it preserves the dataset size. Selecting an appropriate data imputation method is critical for improving a machine learning model's performance.

The following methods are used for data imputation:

1. **Numerical Imputation:** Here you impute the missing value of the numerical data type. For example, if you have a column that

shows the "customer visit count in the last month", the missing values can be replaced with 0, which is a sensible solution. However, the best imputation method is to use the median of the column. Column mean can be used for imputation, but it is more sensitive to outliers.

```
#Filling all missing values with 0
data = data.fillna(0)
#Filling missing values with medians of the columns
data = data.fillna(data.median())|
```

Figure 10: *Pandas fillna() Method*

2. **Categorical Imputation:** In categorial imputation, you find the category which appeared maximum number of times on the given feature and use it on the missing rows. Replacing the missing values with the maximum value in a column is a good option for handling categorical columns. But if the values in the column are distributed uniformly and there is no single dominant value, imputing a category value like "Other" might be more sensible.

```
#Max fill function for categorical columns
data['column_name'].fillna(data['column_name'].value_counts()
.idxmax(), inplace=True)
```

Figure 11: *Pandas fillna() Method for Categorical Column*

Outliers

The best way to detect outliers is to look at the data visually. Visualizing the outliers enables high-precision decision-making. Statistical methodologies are less precise, but they are fast.

1. **Outlier Detection with Standard Deviation:** If a value has a distance to the average higher than $x \times$ Standard Deviation, it can be assumed to be an outlier. x can be between 2 and 4.

```
#Dropping the outlier rows with standard deviation
factor = 3
upper_lim = data['column'].mean () + data['column'].std () * factor
lower_lim = data['column'].mean () - data['column'].std () * factor

data = data[(data['column'] < upper lim) & (data['column'] > lower lim)]
```

Figure 12: *Dropping Outliers with Standard Deviation*

2. **Outlier Detection with Percentiles:** In this method, we assume a certain percentage of the value from the top or the bottom of the feature as an outlier. The key is to set the most appropriate percentage value which depends on the distribution of the dataset.

```
#Dropping the outlier rows with Percentiles
upper_lim = data['column'].quantile(.95)
lower_lim = data['column'].quantile(.05)

data = data[(data['column'] < upper_lim) & (data['column'] > lower_lim)]
```

Figure 13: *Dropping Outliers with Percentiles*

3. **An Outlier Dilemma – To Drop or Cap:** Another option for handling outliers is to cap them instead of dropping them. This way, you can retain your entire dataset, which might be better for the overall model performance. On the other hand, capping can affect the distribution of the data, thus, it is better not to exaggerate it.

```
#Capping the outlier rows with Percentiles
upper_lim = data['column'].quantile(.95)
lower_lim = data['column'].quantile(.05)
data.loc[(df[column] > upper_lim),column] = upper_lim
data.loc[(df[column] < lower_lim),column] = lower_lim
```

Figure 14: *Capping Outliers with Percentiles*

Binning

Binning prevents overfitting and makes the model more robust by reducing non-linearity, irregularities, or noise in the dataset. However, binning can result in performance degradation if not carefully conducted. Every time you bin feature values, you sacrifice information and make your data more regularized. Binning can be applied to numerical and categorical data. The trade-off between performance and overfitting is the key point to consider in the binning process.

```
#Numerical Binning Example
Value       Bin
0-30    ->  Low
31-70   ->  Mid
71-100  ->  High

#Categorical Binning Example
Value       Bin
Spain   ->  Europe
Italy   ->  Europe
Chile   ->  South America
Brazil  ->  South America
```

Figure 15: *Numerical and Categorical Binning Example*

One-Hot Encoding

It is the most commonly used encoding method in machine learning. This method spreads the values of a categorical column to multiple flag/dummy columns and assigns 0 or 1 to them. A categorical variable contains different categories or options for a data feature in the form of string values rather than numeric values. One-hot encoding creates several additional features which are the binary representations of that categorical feature.

One-hot encoding changes categorical data to a numerical format and enables categorical data grouping without losing any information.

For example, let's say that you want to categorize letters [a, b, c, d, e]. To do this, you can use a $n \times 5$ matrix to show the output, where n is the number of individual outputs. If you have an input that gives out [a] then your output matrix will look like [1,0,0,0,0], for [b] it will be [0,1,0,0,0], for [c] it will look like [0,0,1,0,0], and so on.

Scaling

Numerical features have different scales or ranges of values. For example, age and income features cannot have the same range. But from a machine learning perspective, we must align their ranges before modeling. Scaling solves this problem. This process is not mandatory for many algorithms, but it is a good practice to apply for achieving better model performance. However, algorithms based on distance calculations such as k-NN or k-Means need to have scaled continuous features as model inputs.

Two common methods for scaling are:

1. **Normalization** or min-max scaling transforms or rescales the data range between 0 and 1. Normalization is usually applied to features that do not follow the standard Gaussian distribution. However, before applying normalization, always remove outliers because normalization decreases the standard deviation of the dataset, which increases the effect of outliers within the data distribution, eventually resulting in the degradation of the model's performance.

$$X\_norm = \frac{X\_norm}{X\_max - X\_min}$$

```
import pandas as pd
data = pd.DataFrame({'value':[12,32, -11, 45, 28, 2, 95, -20]})

data['normalized'] = (data['value'] - data['value'].min()) / (data['value'].max() - data['value'].min())
print(data)
```

```
   value  normalized
0     12    0.278261
1     32    0.452174
2    -11    0.078261
3     45    0.565217
4     28    0.417391
5      2    0.191304
6     95    1.000000
7    -20    0.000000
```

Figure 16: *Example of Normalization in Python*

2. **Standardization** scales the values via standard deviation. Standardization makes your data robust to outliers, and it ensures all the features are at the same scale. All the elements center around the mean with one standard deviation unit (−1, +1). In the following standardization formula, the mean is shown as , and the standard deviation is shown as σ.

$$z = \frac{x - \mu}{\sigma}$$

```
data = pd.DataFrame({'value':[12,32, -11, 45, 28, 2, 95, -20]})
data['standardized'] = (data['value'] - data['value'].mean()) / data['value'].std()
print(data)

   value  standardized
0     12     -0.297704
1     32      0.249798
2    -11     -0.927330
3     45      0.605673
4     28      0.140297
5      2     -0.571455
6     95      1.974427
7    -20     -1.173706
```

Figure 17: *Example of Standardization in Python*

Feature engineering is an important aspect of machine learning which can't be ignored. Even automated methodologies like AutoML requires engineered features based on the data type, domain, and the problem being solved. Do not forget **"Garbage in, Garbage out!"**

2.4 SUMMARY

- Artificial intelligence and machine learning are data-hungry domains. Data must be refined to improve machine learning predictive capabilities by identifying important features in the data and using them for training better models.

- Exploratory data analysis (EDA) is conducted in the pre-processing phase of machine learning model development.

- EDA can discover unique patterns and detect anomalies in the data with the help of data visualization using matplotlib and seaborn.

- After collecting the dataset, the data pipeline includes data wrangling, feature extraction, feature engineering, feature scaling, feature selection, and dimensionality reduction.

- Feature engineering is meant to extract high-quality data features from raw datasets.

- Different datasets require the use of different feature engineering techniques based on the types of data features.

- Feature engineering techniques usually include data imputation, outlier detection, binning, one-hot encoding, and scaling.
- Robust feature engineering results in high-quality machine learning models.

You should definitely check out the GitHub repository for this chapter to help you understand this section better.

https://github.com/a-soundhararajan/machine-learning/tree/main/Data

There is additional content on my website https://letsbecomemlengineers.com/ and YouTube channel (https://www.youtube.com/channel/UcxxGU_Q6A-8aJlSGP19FYUA), I highly recommend that you check it out.

CHAPTER 3

Training

Model Training & Evaluation Metrics

Now that you have world-class data, next comes the process of training a model to accurately predict the output. You may be getting impatient to learn about the fascinating machine learning algorithms – supervised, unsupervised etc. Don't worry, we're getting there shortly. Let's first discuss the training process and the problems you may encounter during training.

3.1 THE TRAINING PROCESS

The model's training lies at the core of the machine learning process. Machine learning is all about experimenting with the appropriate set of features in order to generate potential models for a particular problem. The majority of "learning" occurs during the training phase. Here, you educate the model using a portion of the dataset that is designated for training. Then you return to the problem's central aim and pick the optimal model (the solution). This model is subject to change as the data changes. It is a constant process; there is no such thing as a completed and flawless model or a set of static facts.

The first thing you do is collect data. This takes the most amount of time, then you move on to the training phase where you will spend most of your time and effort fine-tuning the model's accuracy. It's a lengthy process of trial-and-error; there is no definite answer here.

During the training phase, you choose a validation technique. This technique helps validate your model, analyze the results, and score your model. This procedure is repeated until you are pleased with the model's performance.

3.2 SPLITTING THE DATASET

It's common to split the data into two, even three subsets like the following:

- Training data
- Test data
- Validation data

3.2.1 Why Do You Split the Data?

Let's say that you use all of your data to train your model. After you finish training the model, you want to test it to see if the model you have trained is any good. When you test it with the data that you have already used, it will always give a perfect score in the performance metric that you are using to evaluate the model. Why? Because the model has seen all the different cases already in the training process, so now, no matter what part of the same data you use to test your model with, it will have a perfect score. Your model remembers the training data, or worse, it might have overfit the training dataset.

Model robustness cannot be determined based on previous occurrences encountered by the model. It's the unseen data which defines the accuracy of the model. As a result, you must explicitly split the data for training and model validation.

3.3 TRAINING DATA SPLIT TECHNIQUES

This section explains the different types of dataset splits and how they impact the training process.

3.3.1 Train, and Test Dataset

Typically, 80% of the data is used to train the model (training dataset). Your model's performance will be evaluated using the remaining 20% of the data, the test dataset. The model will not have access to the test dataset during training.

To deliver the best model, you need to perform a lot of training cycles. Out of all the models trained, you validate it using the test dataset to choose the best-performing model.

3.3.2 Train, Validation, and Test Dataset

In this case there are 3 distinct datasets. You will use the training dataset to train the model; the validation, and test datasets are used to evaluate the model. In this case only the training dataset changes the hyperparameters of the model, while validation, and test datasets cannot interact with the model in any meaningful way except for the fact that they provide you with unbiased results of the model.

The training data will be used to train a variety of models, and in each iteration of training you will use the validation dataset to check if the model is overfitting or not. If the model starts overfitting the training dataset, prematurely end the training session. The test dataset is used in the end after you finish training the model to check how good the model performs overall.

You may split the data into 80%-10%-10% for training, validation, and test dataset, respectively.

3.4 HYPERPARAMETER TUNING

A model is like a machine where there are a lot of small knobs for you to tune. When you tune one knob, the output might look different, and it might change a little bit when you tune the other knob. This can become very complicated very fast.

All these knobs are called hyperparameters. A hyperparameter can be the learning rate, number of layers, number of nodes in neural networks, it can be the slope 'm' in linear regression or 'k' in k-nearest neighbors.

You are in control of most of these hyperparameters and finding the best hyperparameter is usually based on trial-and-error.

3.5 TYPES OF MODEL EVALUATION METRICS

We talked about choosing the best model based on model training and testing results. You might be thinking, "what are the metrics used to evaluate and compare the model results?"

A separate set of evaluation metrics is used for various types of challenges. To evaluate machine learning (ML) models, it is crucial to choose the proper measure. A single metric may not provide you with enough information to solve your issue in some instances. You may need to combine it with a few other relevant ones to arrive at a highly accurate model in all potential instances.

Let's look at the different evaluation metrics for the traditional classification and regression problems:

1. Classification
   a. Classification Accuracy
   b. Precision and Recall
   c. F_1 -Score
   d. ROC and AUC Curve

2. Regression
   a. Mean Squared Error and RMSE
   b. Mean Absolute Error
   c. R Square and Adjusted R Square

3.6 EVALUATION METRIC VS. LOSS FUNCTION

If you remember, we said that a loss function is used when training a model to compare the model output and the actual output, and it is ultimately used to perform backpropagation. Now, why do we need to use evaluation metrics if the loss function already performs that function?

The answer is that loss functions are harder to understand compared to the evaluation metrics. When you say this model has 0.0012 loss as compared to saying that this model has 99.9% accuracy, we immediately see which one of those is more understandable. Loss functions are solely useful for backpropagation and are differentiable, evaluation metrics serve a different purpose.

3.7 CONFUSION MATRIX

A confusion matrix is a tabular depiction of the connection between model predictions and ground-truth labels. Each row of the confusion matrix represents an actual class, and each column represents a predicted class.

Let's go through this with an example and build a binary classification to separate cat images from non-cat images. Let's assume our test set has 1000 images (350 cat images and 650 non-cat ones), with the below confusion matrix.

Total=1000	Predicted — YES	Predicted — NO
Actual — YES	300	70
Actual — NO	80	625

There are 4 essential terms to understand here,

1. True Positives: The cases in which we predicted YES, and the actual output was also YES (**300**).

2. True Negatives: The cases in which we predicted NO, and the actual output was NO (**625**).

3. False Positives: The cases in which we predicted YES, and the actual output was NO (**70**).

4. False Negatives: The cases in which we predicted NO, and the actual output was YES (**80**).

In this matrix, we can observe that diagonal components correspond to accurate predictions for distinct classes, and the off-diagonal elements correspond to samples that were incorrectly categorized in each class.

3.8 CLASSIFICATION METRICS

Choosing the correct evaluation metric is critical for analyzing the expected class vs. actual class outcomes and making the necessary changes in the training process to improve the model prediction rate. Accuracy, precision, recall, and F1-score are well-known classification evaluation metrics. Confusion matrix is the foundation of all the classification metrics.

3.8.1 Classification Accuracy

Classification accuracy is the simplest statistic to measure. It is given by the formula:

$$Classification\ Accuracy = \frac{Number\ of\ Correct\ Predictions}{Total\ Number\ of\ Forecasts}$$

It gives you a percentage of correct predictions. To understand all of the different classification metrics we will use a simple example. Say you have 100 students. 80 of them are boys and 20 of them are girls. You have a model that predicts the gender of the students. If your model assigns literally every input as a male, your model will have 80% classification accuracy.

The keen-eyed amongst you might have noticed that although you have an 80% accuracy it is clearly a very bad model. Classification accuracy made your model appear better than it actually is. This is why you should not be using classification accuracy when your classes are imbalanced (like 80 males, and 20 females in this example). Accuracy is a great metric to use when you have your classes equally balanced.

3.8.2 Precision and Recall

If a model's distribution of classes is not equal, then it might give a false positive result when you use the classification accuracy.

This is why we have metrics called precision and recall. Precision is given by the following formula:

$$Precision = \frac{True\ Positive}{True\ Positive + False\ Positive}$$

Precision gives you the ratio of the correctly classified outcomes of a single class to the total outcomes classified as that class. To illustrate this, let's say that you want to find the precision of the model you created to find the gender of the students. It will go as follows:

$$Precision\ in\ classifying\ male = \frac{80}{80 + 0} = 1$$

$$Precision\ in\ classifying\ female = \frac{0}{0 + 20} = 0$$

What we learn from this metric is that your model is the most precise when predicting males, but it could not be more wrong when predicting females.

Recall is given by the following formula:

$$Recall = \frac{True\ Positive}{True\ Positive + False\ Negative}$$

$$Recall\ in\ classifying\ male\ = \frac{80}{80 + 20} = 0.80$$

$$Recall\ in\ classifying\ female\ = \frac{0}{0 + 80} = 0$$

Recall gives a ratio of the correct classifications of a class to the wrong ones. Again, let's go back to your model:

This metric shows you that your model classifies so many inputs as males that it only achieves 80% accuracy in the class of males.

3.8.3 F1 Score

The importance of recall and precision might vary greatly depending on the application. When it comes to many instances, recall is more important than precision. Consequently, the question of how to combine these two indicators into a single metric is warranted. The F_1-score, which is defined as the harmonic mean of precision and recall and may be computed as follows, is a popular metric that incorporates both accuracy and memory. The F_1-score value ranges from 0 to 1.

$$F_1 = 2 \cdot \frac{Precision \times Recall}{Precision + Recall}$$

In our example, the F_1-score is:

$$F_1\ male\ = 2 \cdot \frac{1 \times 0.8}{1 + 0.8} = 0.88$$

$$F_1\ female\ = 2 \cdot \frac{0 \times 0}{0 + 0} = 0$$

There is always a trade-off between precision and recall in a model, and if you wish to make the precision very high, you'll observe a decline in the recall rate, and vice versa.

3.9 REGRESSION METRICS

In the regression problem, we are predicting a numerical value, for example, we are predicting a house price or used car value. Unlike classification problems, we cannot use classification accuracy in regression scenarios. We have error metrics to evaluate the regression models.

3.9.1 Mean Squared Error and RMSE

The mean squared error (MSE) is the most often used statistic for regression situations. It is primarily concerned with determining the average squared error between the anticipated and observed values.

$$MSE = \frac{1}{N} \sum_{i=1}^{N} (y_i - \hat{y}_i)^2$$

Root mean squared error (RMSE) is the square root of the MSE. When compared to mean absolute error (MAE), the benefit of mean squared error is that it is simpler to calculate the gradient. MAE requires complicated linear programming tools to compute the gradient.

3.9.2 Mean Absolute Error

Mean absolute error is the measure of distance between the expected and target values. It provides us with an indication of how far off the forecasts were from the actual outcome. This measure does not provide any indication of the direction in which we are making errors, that is, whether we are underpredicting or overpredicting the data.

$$MAE = \frac{1}{N} \sum_{i=1}^{N} |y_i - \hat{y}_i|$$

MAE is more robust to outliers than MSE. By squaring the errors in MSE, the outliers (which often have bigger errors than the data points) get more attention and dominance in the final error, which has an influence on the model parameters.

3.9.3 R2 and Adjusted R2

The smaller the root mean square error (RMSE), the better the model will perform. Our model's performance may be judged by comparing it to a generic model, which has an accuracy of 0.5 in a classification problem.

Thus, the generic model can be utilized as a starting point or a benchmark. We don't have a reference to compare the RMSE measurements against though.

This is where we can use R^2 metric. We have a baseline value to compare against which is not the not case in other metrics. The formula for R^2 is as follows:

MSE (model): Mean squared error of the predictions against the actual values.
MSE (baseline): Mean squared error of the mean prediction against the actual values.

$$R^2 = 1 - \frac{MSE(model)}{MSE(baseline)}$$

R^2 would be 0 if the model was performing exactly like the baseline. The greater the R^2 score, the more accurate the model. R^2 would be 1 if all forecasts were right, according to the best model.

$$\overline{R^2} = 1 - (1 - R^2)\frac{n - 1}{n - (k + 1)}$$

On adding new features to the model, the R^2 value either increases or remains the same. R^2 does not penalize us for adding features that add no value to the model. So, an improved version over the R^2 is the adjusted R^2.

Where, k is the number of features, and is the number of samples.

If R^2 does not increase, the added feature isn't valuable for our model. So, overall, we subtract a greater value from 1 and the adjusted R^2, in turn, would decrease.

While most of these evaluation metrics originate from the statistical realm, there is another effective machine learning strategy for evaluating model performance. It is none other than the cross-validation technique.

Cross validation is not an accurate evaluation metric to indicate the model's accuracy. However, the outcome of cross validation offers a sufficient intuitive conclusion to generalize a model's performance.

3.10 CROSS VALIDATION

Cross validation is a critical concept in any kind of data modelling, and it is especially important in statistical modelling. It is used to evaluate machine learning models on a limited data sample. It uses unseen data to estimate the accuracy of a machine learning model.

The disadvantage of this strategy is that we lose a significant quantity of data throughout the model training process. As a result, the model has a very high level of bias. And cross validation will not provide the most accurate estimation of the coefficients.

Let's take a look at a type of cross validation called k-fold cross validation.

3.10.1 k-fold Cross Validation

The k-fold cross validation divides the dataset into number of sets and utilize number of sets to train the model and $k - n$ number of sets to test the model. You will understand it much better with the example below:

You have a dataset like this: [0, 1, 2, 3, 4, 5, 6, 7, 8, 9]

You choose a k of 5, and so the algorithm makes 5 groups of numbers for the dataset like the following:

$fold_1 = [0,1]$; $fold_2 = [2,5]$; $fold_3 = [9,6]$; $fold_4 = [3,7]$; $fold_5 = [4,8]$

Now that we have 5 folds, we can use any of the 4 folds to train and 1 fold to test the model. It will be something like:

- Model 1: Trained on folds 2, 3, 4, 5. Tested on fold 1.
- Model 2: Trained on folds 1, 3, 4, 5. Tested on fold 2.
- Model 3: Trained on folds 1, 2, 4, 5. Tested on fold 3.
- Model 4: Trained on folds 1, 2, 3, 5. Tested on fold 4.
- Model 5: Trained on folds 1, 2, 3, 4. Tested on fold 5.

You will need to try this for every model and pick the model that performs the best.

The general procedure is as follows:

- Shuffle the dataset randomly.
- Split the dataset into k groups.
- For each unique group:
  - Take the group as a holdout or test dataset.
  - Take the remaining groups as training datasets.
  - Fit a model on the training set and evaluate it on the test set.
  - Retain the evaluation score and discard the model.
- Summarize the accuracy of the model using the sample of model evaluation scores.

How do we choose k? That is the tricky part; we have a trade-off to choose k. For a small k, we have a higher selection bias but a low variance in the performances. For a large k, we have a small selection bias but a high variance in the performances.

There is no strict rule for what the number of k should be, however, it is generally between 5 and 10. Because of this, as k increases, it becomes more difficult to distinguish between the training and resampling sets. With a smaller gap, the technique's bias becomes smaller as well.

Generally, a value of $k = 10$ is recommended for most purposes.

3.11 CHALLENGES IN TRAINING MODELS

3.11.1 Lack of Training Data

Machine learning models are data-hungry, and their success is highly dependent on the amount of training data available. Even a primary cat versus dog categorization job takes at least 1000s of photos. Machine learning solutions for complex problems such as image classification and speech recognition need millions of data samples. Google, Amazon, and Facebook all have the data they need to address their issues.

However, small businesses rely heavily on transactional data and are always looking for new data sources. In some cases, they may already have the data, for example, patient data in healthcare, but they cannot use it for training purposes unless they get the necessary consent and comply with applicable legislation. Inadequate training data is a reasonably prevalent issue that businesses are now facing. Several open-source repositories, such as the www.kaggle.com / UCI Machine Learning repository and the Google dataset, contain freely accessible public datasets. The ImageNet dataset is an excellent starting point for developing picture classification or object identification algorithms.

3.11.2 Non-representative Training Data

The training dataset should include all instances that have happened and are likely to occur. If the number of training samples is insufficient, you will have sampling noise or non-representative data. If you train your model on a non-representative training set, the prediction accuracy will be lower, and the model will be biased towards a certain class or group.

The first versions of Amazon and Google's voice assistant applications are notable instances of this issue, they were unable to distinguish non-native English speakers. When selecting training dataset samples for your model, ensure that you include samples from all population segments; this will help your model generalize effectively to previously unknown data.

3.11.3 Over-fitting of Training Data

The model works well during training but struggles with new data. Over-fitting occurs when the model is too complicated. The model learns the correlations in the training data and the noise to the point where it has a detrimental effect on the model's performance on new data.

High test error implies over-fitting, which you can avoid by:

- Selecting a model with fewer features. This prefers a more linear model compared to a higher degree polynomial model.
- Fixing data errors, removing the outliers, and reducing the number of samples in the training set.

3.11.4 Under-fitting of Training Data

In this case, the model is trained with insufficient data and it is too simplistic to comprehend the connections contained within the data. The model does not suit all cases and so fails to train. High training error implies under-fitting, which you can avoid by:

- Choosing an advanced model with additional parameters.
- Train on relevant features.

3.12 SUMMARY

- Model training is the core machine learning process; it produces a functional model that can then be validated, tested, and deployed.
- It is common to split the dataset into training and test sets or training, validation, and test sets. Validation and test sets used to evaluate the trained model without bias.
- Confusion matrix is the foundation of all the classification metrics. Accuracy, precision, recall, and F1-score are well-known classification evaluation metrics.
- Regression models use error metrics for evaluation. MSE, MAE and R^2 are widely used regression evaluation metrics.

- Cross validation technique can be used to get a quick understanding on model's accuracy.
- Irrespective of the machine learning approach you take either statistical method vs. neural networks, the training problems — lack of data, non-representative data, and overfitting or underfitting will need to be addressed.

If you made it this far, you should go ahead to the GitHub repository made specifically for this chapter to practically implement everything that you have learnt till now.

https://github.com/a-soundhararajan/machine-learning/tree/main/Training

There is additional content on my website https://letsbecomemlengineers.com/ and YouTube channel (https://www.youtube.com/channel/UcxxGU_Q6A-8aJlSGP19FYUA), I highly recommend that you check it out.

CHAPTER 4

Foundations

Five Pillars of Machine Learning

In this chapter, we will discuss the foundational aspects of machine learning. Topics such as statistics, probability, linear algebra, calculus, and the gradient descent algorithm will be covered.

Machine learning is mainly mathematics, so we cannot hide from math. Although you do not need a degree in mathematics, there are some simple concepts that you should be familiar with before you start to really understand machine learning. Statistics and probability are used to explore the data that you have. Linear algebra, calculus, and partial derivatives are the foundations of machine learning algorithms.

All the concepts in this chapter are things you have learnt in high school, and if you do not remember them, then this chapter will be a perfect refresher. I have also added some great YouTube content below if you want to dive deep into the math. If you really do not like math, then you can merely skim through the chapter and familiarize yourself with the terminologies and concepts.

4.1 STATISTICS

Statisticians use all the tools at their disposal to find patterns in their data and extract insights from the data. There are 2 types of statistical tools available, descriptive statistics and inferential statistics.

4.1.1 Descriptive Statistics

A dataset can have thousands or millions of data points. Descriptive statistics is a way to make the data more understandable to human beings. It aims to simplify all the data into a few data points so that you can understand it better. It is not concerned with learning from the data, only summarizing the information from the dataset.

For example, you have the date and frequency of births in a country categorized state-wise. If you find the average birthrate in a year or find the average age of women giving birth, then such analysis is called descriptive statistics. In this example, you are summarizing the information of birth in 1 or 2 numbers, and you are not making any predictions regarding births.

Now you might be thinking, why is this useful when this whole book is about predicting things? This is usually the first step when you start on a machine learning project as discussed in Chapter 2. When you explore the data, you are learning about the dataset as it is. You are not trying to force anything to happen, you are not trying to fit models in your data or use the data to make predictions. You might have a pre-conceived notion about the data before you start, and sometimes those thoughts might be wrong. Exploring these datasets can help you correct yourself if your initial conclusions are wrong.

Many people neglect this step, but it is highly recommended that you perform this step first as it will help you immensely. It will sometimes bring to your notice the possible outliers, as well as prepare you for hypothesis testing and ML models fitting.

Now let's explore the descriptive statistics in detail.

Mean

The mean is the average value of your dataset. This is the single best value to represent your data. You can think of this as the middle value of the whole dataset. It is calculated using every value present in your data. A disadvantage of the mean is that it is vulnerable to the outliers in the dataset. If you have one value that is very large or very small compared to others, the mean is affected accordingly.

The equation of the mean is shown below:

$$\bar{x} = \frac{\sum x_i}{n}$$

So, basically you add all the datapoints and divide this value by the total number of data points.

For example, for a dataset of [60, 20, 10, 40, 50, 30]:

$$\bar{x} = \frac{\sum x_i}{n} = \frac{60 + 20 + 10 + 40 + 50 + 30}{6}$$

$$\bar{x} = 35$$

To illustrate the outlier disadvantage, let's add the value 1000 to the dataset, making it [60, 20, 10, 40, 50, 30, 1000]

$$\bar{x} = \frac{\sum x_i}{n} = \frac{60 + 20 + 10 + 40 + 50 + 30 + 1000}{7}$$

$$\bar{x} = 172.85$$

As you can see, when we added an outlier data point to the dataset, the mean of the whole dataset changed drastically. You should keep an eye out for outliers when you use this function.

Median

Median is the value that is exactly in the middle of the complete dataset. The value should be such that 50% of the dataset is on either side of the value. Median is not affected by the presence of outliers, but it does not consider all the data points that you have in your dataset.

To find the median of the dataset, you need to sort it in an ascending order and choose the middle element. If there are 2 middle digits, then you need to find the mean of the 2 values.

For example, for a dataset of [10, 20, 30, 40, 50, 60], the median is 35.

Let's add an outlier to the data and find the median. For the dataset [10, 20, 30, 40, 50, 60, 1000], the median is 40.

Mode

The mode of your data is the value that occurs the greatest number of times in the dataset. The mode is not ideal for continuous data that can take any value within a range of values.

For example, in the voting process, the mode is the candidate's name that is repeated the most. So, the mode number corresponds to the winner of the election.

Let's say we have candidates like below:

Candidate	Alice	Felix	Sean	Paul	Tim	Bobby
Votes	60	20	10	40	50	30

The mode in this dataset is 60, which corresponds to Alice who won the election.

The mean and median are measures of central tendency and are unique values. The mode may not be unique, and you can have more than one mode for a dataset. In the election above, if two candidates get the same number of votes then both are winners of the election.

Measures of Dispersion

Dispersion is the measure of how spread out the data is.

Now we will explore some measures of dispersion.

Range

This value is represented by the difference between the maximum and minimum values in a dataset. Range is very sensitive to the presence of outliers.

Variance

The variance is an averaged measure of how much a data point deviates from the mean of a dataset.

It is shown by the following formula:

$$S^2 = \frac{\Sigma(x_i - \bar{x})^2}{n - 1}$$

Where S is the variance, $\bar{x}$ is the mean, and n is the total number of points. If you look at the formula closely, you will notice that the variance is simply the sum of the squares of the mean deviations divided by the number of data points you have in your data.

Standard Deviation

Standard deviation is the square root of variance.

$$\sigma = \sqrt{\frac{\Sigma(x_1 - \mu)^2}{N}}$$

You might notice that the formula for standard deviation and variance is very similar. You are not alone. But there is a difference in how the two measures are used. Variance is used to find the distribution of data in a population from a mean, and standard deviation also helps to know the distribution of data in a population, but the difference between the two is that standard deviation gives more clarity about the deviation of the data from the mean. To understand better, look at the Figure 1 below:

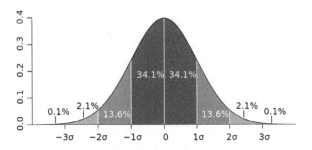

Figure 1: *Standard Deviation [1]*

In the x-axis you will notice 0, 1σ, 2σ, 3σ. They are the standard deviations. Take the example of IQ, if a person's IQ is between 85-115 then they are 1 standard deviation above or below the mean. If you take a look at the above graph, 1 standard deviation means 68.2% of the total dataset. That is, 68.2% of all people have an IQ in the range of 85-115. 95% of all people will have an IQ score within 2 standard deviations of the mean (between 70 – 130).

Inter-Quartile Range

This value is the difference between the 75th percentile and the 25th percentile of the data. It is shown below:

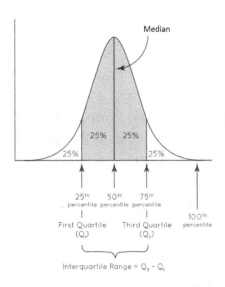

Figure 2: *Inter-quartile Range [2]*

4.2 PROBABILITY

Probability is the chance of an event occurring. It is measured as follows:

$$Probability\ of\ an\ event\ = \frac{Number\ ways\ an\ event\ can\ occur}{Total\ number\ of\ possible\ outcomes}$$

For example, if you are tossing a coin, then the probability of getting heads is 0.5. This means that you will get heads half the time and not-heads (tails), the other half.

Gaussian Distribution

This is also called the normal distribution. This is a method in which you can present your data. In this type of distribution, the data is represented by the graph shown in Figure 2 where the center of the graph represents the mean of the whole dataset. Then, 68% of the data points lie in 1 standard deviation of the mean, and so on, as shown in Figure 1.

4.3 LINEAR ALGEBRA

Linear algebra is the backbone of machine learning. You need to learn linear algebra because it is applied in all areas of machine learning, including linear regression, loss functions, singular value decomposition (SVD), support vector machine (SVM), and a lot more.

Linear Equation

A linear equation is an equation in the form of

$$y = mx + b$$

Where y, x are variables, m is the slope, and b is the y-intercept. The keen-eyed amongst you might recognize this equation as the equation of a straight line.

Vectors

A vector is a one-dimensional array of numbers.

For example, [0, 1]

Matrix

A matrix is a two-dimensional array of numbers. It is a group of numbers arranged in rows and columns.

For example, $\begin{bmatrix} 0 & 1 \\ 2 & 3 \end{bmatrix}$

Tensors

Tensor is exactly like a matrix except for the part that tensors are objects. Tensors are used in neural networks to store calculated values.

4.4 CALCULUS

You might have learnt in school what calculus is. It is the mathematical study of continuous change.

What is a continuous change? It is an ongoing, gradual change that doesn't stop at a specific value. If you think of the speed of a car, a car does not stop in time to give you a value saying, "my speed is 30 miles per hour". A car's speed changes continuously in time.

In calculus, you need to know about the derivative of a function. Let's consider a function like the graph below:

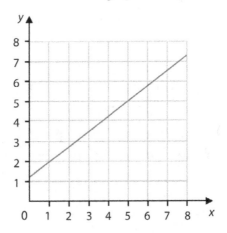

Figure 3: *A Linear Graph [3]*

The derivative calculates the slope of a graph in an instantaneous point in time. Continuing the previous example of the car, you are basically stopping the car in time and calculating the speed at that moment. To find the speed of the car, we need the speed formula:

$$Speed = \frac{Distance}{Time}$$

You can write that in a fancy way as follows:

$$s = f(d,t) = \frac{dd}{dt}$$

The $\frac{dd}{dt}$ in the equation above is the derivative of distance d with respect to time t. This equation also equates $f(d, t)$ with speed, which means that speed is a function of (d, t). This denotes that speed depends on distance and time. Which makes sense because if you cover a lot of distance in a short time then the speed increases, but if you cover the same amount of distance in a long stretch of time then the speed decreases.

In the above example, we are lucky that we can only control the distance in time, and not time itself. If we could control time, then there would be new questions that we need to answer. Questions like, what would the speed be if you stop time and cover a lot of distance, what would the speed be if you stop covering distance and let time run for a long time, and the other variations of these questions. To answer all these questions, we would need to find a new way to explain how speed works. But what if we could really control time? To answer this question, we have another area of calculus called partial derivative.

Partial Derivative

Let's forget about speed and time for this concept because we cannot control time no matter how hard we try. Let's look at the distribution of heat in a room in Figure 4.

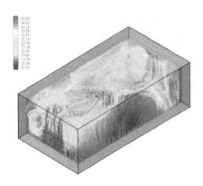 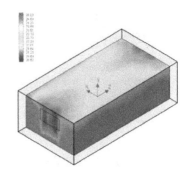

Figure 4: *Room Temperature Distribution Map [4]*

If you look at the graphs above and try to model the temperature, you will see that the temperature of the room depends on the *x*, *y*, *z* position in the room. You could say that if you stand in the red areas marked in the graph, you will be warmer, and you will be cooler in the blue regions. Luckily, the above graph gives us the temperature at an instant in time, otherwise the graph would be moving (also known as a video), and it would make things very difficult.

We will model this concept with an example:

$$Temperature = f(x, y, z)$$

Now that we know about the graph, the questions the partial derivative was created to answer are the following:

How would the temperature change if I moved in the *x* direction of this room and not in *y* or *z* directions?

$$Temperature\ change\ along\ x\ direction = \frac{\delta f(x, y, z)}{\delta x}$$

How would the temperature change if I moved in the *y* direction of this room and not in *x* or *z* directions?

$$Temperature\ change\ along\ y\ direction = \frac{\delta f(x, y, z)}{\delta y}$$

How would the temperature change if I moved in the z direction of this room and not in x or y directions?

$$\textit{Temperature change along z direction} = \frac{\delta f(x, y, z)}{\delta z}$$

If you looked closely at the above questions, then you must have observed that the values of 2 variables were kept constant and one variable was changed to find its slope in each of the questions. This function is very similar to the linear function, and the derivative calculates the slope of the graph.

Applying the Mathematical Concepts to Machine Learning: Enough about temperature and velocity of cars, how does this apply to machine learning? To use these concepts in relation to machine learning, you need to know that machine learning or deep learning algorithms have parameters that you can tune. Tuning these parameters helps the models become better over time. Derivatives come into the picture for this specific purpose.

$$\frac{\delta \textit{Loss function}(x, y)}{\delta(x)}$$

Derivative of the loss function with respect to a specific parameter (as shown in the equation above) tells you how to tune the parameter so that your model's loss function is minimized. Just the way you know how the temperature changes in your room and that you can use the 3 partial derivatives to walk to the coldest region of your room, the partial derivative of the loss function with respect to the parameter under consideration will lead the model to the point where the loss is minimum.

The only concept you should know is the concept of slope and the fact that a positive slope means that the value is increasing in the graph, and a negative slope means the value is decreasing in the graph.

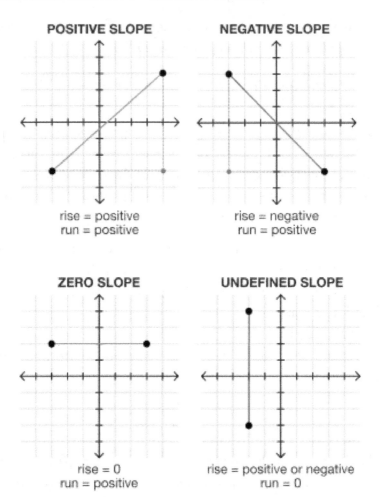

Figure 5: *Slopes and their Respective Graphs [5]*

4.1.5 Sources to Deep Dive

If you are not satisfied with just knowing the above concepts at the surface level, then you should dive deeper into the subjects.

Here are some recommendations:

- Statistics: https://www.youtube.com/watch?v=VPZD_aij8H0
- Probability: https://www.youtube.com/watch?v=EObHWIEKGjA
- Linear Algebra – https://www.youtube.com/watch?v=k0zKoTvngUY

- Multivariate Calculus – https://www.youtube.com/watch?v=bCx6UuzXPA0

Once you understand the math behind the machine learning algorithms, you will be able to differentiate among the various algorithms and choose the best algorithm for the data you have.

Now we will learn about the most important concept when it comes to machine learning and deep learning.

4.5 GRADIENT DESCENT

Gradient descent is arguably the most important concept in this book. If you want to get a thorough understanding of machine learning, you need to understand gradient descent.

Another name for gradient descent is optimization algorithm. What does it optimize? It is used to optimize the cost function. Almost every machine learning algorithm (be it a statistical or a deep learning algorithm) has an optimization algorithm at its core.

4.2.1 Why Gradient Descent?

When you train a model, the ideal model gives an output with the lowest error rate possible. You can decrease the loss by manually optimizing all the hyperparameters, or by utilizing an optimizing algorithm.

When you use a gradient descent algorithm, it tunes the hyperparameters for you and gives you a model that produces outputs with the lowest losses. The gradient descent takes place under-the-hood and you do not have to write any code for it.

You might be wondering already if optimization is a common theme in machine learning, you are absolutely right. In linear regression, you need to optimize the intercept and the slope. When you use logistic regression, you need to optimize the squiggle part. Even when you are performing clustering in unsupervised learning, you need to optimize the clusters. When you are designing a neural network, you need to optimize the weights and biases in the network. The cool thing is that gradient descent can optimize all these things and more. Now let's dive into the world of gradient descent.

4.2.2 What is Gradient Descent?

The gradient descent algorithm is something we call an iterative first-order optimization algorithm. What it does is finds the local maximum or minimum of a function.

Machine learning algorithms have a loss function that needs to be minimized.

We will now investigate a very, very simplified version of a loss function so you have an idea of how these things work in practice. Take a look at the graph in Figure 6.

$$\text{loss} = f(x) = y = x^2$$

In the graph shown in Figure 6, the loss function is:

In a perfect world, our algorithm should find that $x = 0$ gives us the lowest loss possible y (which is also 0).

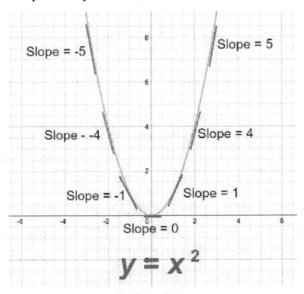

Figure 6: *A Convex Loss Function [6]*

We can do this iteratively by looping the following equation (which is the gradient descent equation):

$$x = x - \lambda \frac{dx}{dy}$$

Where x, y are the points on the graph, and λ is the learning rate. The learning rate defines how much the data point jumps. If the learning rate is too small, then the cost function will never reach the minimum point, and if the learning rate is too high then it will offshoot the minimum point.

Let's see what we get when we solve $\frac{dx}{dy}$:

$$\frac{dy}{dx} = \frac{dx^2}{dx} = 2x$$

Now we can write the final equation as follows:

$$x = x - 2\lambda x$$

It is possible to write a simple script to iterate over this function. The following code is in Python, and you should try it in your own system:

```
import random

x = random.randint(-100, 100)
lr = 0.01
for i in range(1000):
    x -= lr*2*x
    if i % 100 == 0:
        print(x)
```

When you run this snippet of code, then the value of x reaches 0 or very close to 0 in less than 1000 iterations. Hence, it is proven that our function works just like we intended it to work. In the example we glossed over the process of picking the learning rate (lr). The learning rate is the hyperparameter in the function and it is up to you to pick it for yourself. You usually come to a value through trial-and-error. Feel free to change the learning rate in the code above to see how it affects the outcome. You may find that some learning rates will let you converge in fewer iterations, or in a greater number of iterations.

In this example you got an understanding of how a loss function can be minimized by using the gradient descent algorithm. It is actually this simple in neural networks too, but in that case there are a lot of variables and you need to calculate a lot of partial derivatives.

If you are really into the nitty-gritty math of how the neural networks work then you should definitely check out this great video by 3Blue1Brown on YouTube: https://www.youtube.com/watch?v=IHZwWFHWa-w

4.2.3 Loss Function

Mean Squared Error Loss

Also called MSE, this is one of the simplest loss functions. Let's look at its formula:

$$MSE = \frac{1}{n}\sum_{i=1}^{n}(Y_i - \hat{Y}_i)^2$$

where n is the number of data points, Y_i is the observed value, and $\hat{Y}_i$ is the predicted value.

Even though this loss function looks completely different compared to the one in our example, it is actually very similar. In our example we took x to mean 1 data point, but the MSE loss function is intended to be used with a batch of input.

Both the Y_i and $\hat{Y}_i$ are tensors of output. The difference between the actual output and the predicted output is calculated, squared, and the mean of the squares are calculated. When you square the output, you get a very similar graph to that of Figure 6.

So, in the end, even though this equation looks complicated when compared to $y = x^2$, they are very similar. Now you might be thinking, in $y = x^2$ the minimum value of y is 0, so the x will also be 0. What about MSE loss?

To get the minimum value for the MSE loss, the value of $Y_i - \hat{Y}_i$ should be minimized. Or you can say that the model's prediction should be very similar to the actual output.

There are many different loss functions, some of which are cross-entropy loss, negative log-likelihood loss, hinge loss, Huber loss, and a lot more. You should check them out if you are interested in them, but usually with experience you will stumble across these loss functions, and you can learn as you come across them.

4.2.4 Problems with Gradient Descent

If you study the different types of losses, then you might notice that they are all convex functions. What is a convex function anyways? Well, take a look:

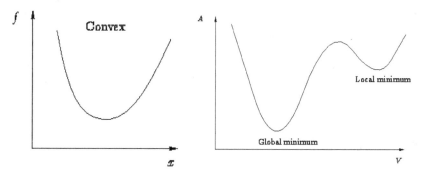

Figure 7: *Convex and Non-Convex Functions [7]*

A convex function only has 1 minima, while a non-convex function has many minima. If the gradient descent gears are turning in your head, you will see how easy it would be to reach a minima in the convex function but it would be very bad in the non-convex function if you get stuck in the local minima.

There are some loss functions that are non-convex and hence, you are very susceptible to get stuck in the local minima and never reach the global minima. This is one problem of the gradient descent.

Another problem with the gradient descent happens when you get stuck in a plateau. The plateau is the point in a graph where the slope is very small, and you are not able to make much progress. It is shown in the figure below:

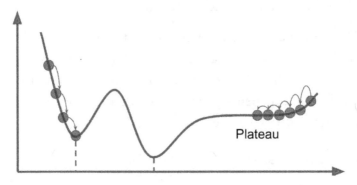

Figure 8: *Showing the Local Minima and the Plateau [8]*

4.2.5 Stochastic Gradient Descent

Regular gradient descent is performed on all the data points. When there are millions of data points, this can be very inefficient. So, there is a type of gradient descent called stochastic gradient descent that applies the gradient descent algorithm on a subset of the data rather than the full dataset.

4.6 SUMMARY

- Statistics is the study of analyzing data to draw a conclusion from it.

- It is very important to explore the dataset that you have on your own. It will help greatly in finding out the intricacies of the dataset that you are working with. Every data is different so you should make a habit of this.

- Descriptive statistic methods are the methods to get an understanding of datasets by summarizing the data points into short digestible forms.

- Machine learning algorithms perform much better when the input features are normally distributed. A normal distribution (also called Gaussian distribution) is a bell-shaped curve that has the middle point as the mean and all other data points lie around this mean.

- Linear algebra, and calculus are very important if you want to get an intuitive understanding of machine learning algorithms.
- Machine learning is overall an optimization process.
- Gradient descent is an optimization algorithm that is used extensively in machine learning.
- Gradient descent can optimize the hyperparameters of a machine learning algorithm for you to give you a model that is very accurate.
- You should be wary of local minima, and plateaus in the loss function when you are implementing gradient descent.

If you have reached this point, I highly recommend you check out the GitHub page of this chapter. You will learn a lot more. https://github.com/a-soundhararajan/machine-learning/tree/main/Foundations

There is additional content on my website https://letsbecomemlengineers.com/ and YouTube channel (https://www.youtube.com/channel/UcxxGU_Q6A-8aJlSGP19FYUA), I highly recommend that you check it out.

CHAPTER 5

Supervised

Learning with a Teacher

Based on my personal experience, learning with a teacher or a coach exponentially accelerates the overall learning process. I am sure we all learned driving with an instructor sitting by our side telling us the dos and don'ts. If there is no one to guide you, then there is no guarantee of the outcome you are going to end up with. This is the basic premise of supervised learning as you will see soon.

5.1 WHAT IS SUPERVISED LEARNING?

Supervised learning is all about having assistance during the learning process. Here the dataset has an output for every input, this output can be seen as a teacher for the model.

There is a manual human intervention to annotate the data sets with expected outcomes for each row. The training process is guided by labels (labels are nothing but the expected outputs). We cannot begin the training process without including these labels in the data in supervised learning.

5.2 SUPERVISED LEARNING ALGORITHMS

Supervised learning algorithms solve regression and classification problems. While some algorithms solve either of these problems, there are a few popular ones which solve both the types.

Linear regression is an algorithm that is used for regression problems.

Logistic regression and naïve Bayes classifier are used for classification problems.

There are some algorithms that can solve both classification and regression problems. Those algorithms are support vector machine, k-nearest neighbors, decision trees, and random forests.

By the end of this chapter, you will see what these algorithms are and know their basics.

5.3 ALGORITHMS FOR REGRESSION

5.3.1 Linear Regression

Linear regression is one of the most well-known algorithms in statistics and machine learning. You might have heard of it, or if you have taken any course in machine learning you might have started out by learning about it. But is it not a technique from statistics?

Linear regression is both a statistical as well as a machine learning algorithm. It is borrowed by machine learning from statistics. It is a model that helps in understanding the relationship between input and output numerical variables.

This model assumes that there is a linear relationship between the input variables and the single output variable y. Hence, the word "linear" in linear regression. In case of a single input variable x, it is called simple linear regression. But if there are multiple input variables, then it is called as multiple linear regression in statistical literature. Needless to say, you should only use this method if you have sufficient proof that the input and output are linear.

The central idea is to get the best fitting line for the data. It is the line for which the total prediction error (all data points) is as small as possible. The best fit line is also called a regression line. The distance between the data point and the regression line is called error.

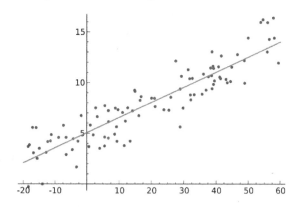

Figure 1: *Line of Best Fit in Linear Regression [1]*

When you feed your data to the regression algorithm, the training process comes up with a hypothesis. A hypothesis is an equation that the model thinks best represents your data – the more you train your model, the more accurate the hypothesis gets but it can also get complicated and overfit the data in the end.

Let's say you trained your model and got a hypothesis like the one shown below:

$$y = mx + c$$

You know that this is the equation of a straight line, where c is the bias and m is the slope of the line or you can call it a parameter. This equation works only when you have 1 independent variable x. What if you have many variables? Then your hypothesis will change to the following:

$$y = m_1x_1 + m_2x_2 + c$$

This equation makes a plane instead of a 2-D line segment. So, you can see how things get complicated very easily when you start to add more variables.

Finding the optimum values for x and m gives you the optimum model. The next step is to check if the output that your model created is actually good or not. How do you do that? By using an error function. An error function (also called a cost function) is a way to find the difference between the output that your model gave you and the actual output that you want from the model. An error function is given by the equation below:

$$J = \frac{1}{n}\sum_{i=1}^{n}(pred_i - y_i)^2$$

where J is the cost function, and y is the actual output.

Let's tie everything together with an example. You have a dataset and you created a model which then predicted the following equation:

$$y = mx + c = 0.9 \times x + 2$$

Now you input $x = 10$ into your equation which then yields:

$$y = 0.9 \times 10 + 2 = 11$$

You check the actual output for $x = 10$, and it is 12 (not 11). You now need to use the cost function to see how much error your model has:

$$J = (pred - y)^2 = (11 - 12)^2 = 1$$

So, you see that your error is 1, you can also see that the error will change exponentially with the difference between the prediction and actual output.

Rules for Linear Regression

As we have already discussed, there needs to be a linear relationship between the input and the output. This algorithm does not work if the relationship is non-linear. Therefore, the first step is to check the linearity of the data before applying this algorithm to it.

The dataset should also be non-noisy without outliers that affect the whole model in a negative way. It is also better if the dataset is normally distributed since the algorithm makes reliable predictions that way. You should also rescale the input variables not only to make it normally distributed but also by standardization so that everything is within a set range (usually 0-1).

Pros and Cons of Linear Regression

The advantage of linear regression is that it is a simple model and is computationally efficient. It does not require complicated calculations and makes predictions fast when the amount of data is large.

The main disadvantage of linear regression is that it assumes that the input and output points are linearly related. This is not always true in real-world scenarios. Another disadvantage of linear regression is that outliers can have a large effect on the output, as the best fit line tries to minimize the mean squared error for the outlier points as well, resulting in a model that is not able to capture the information in the data.

5.4 ALGORITHMS FOR CLASSIFICATION

5.4.1 Logistic Regression

Logistic regression is a simple and efficient method for binary and linear classification problems. It is easy to understand and achieves good performance with linearly separable classes. It is an extensively used algorithm for classification problems in the industry.

The major difference between linear and logistic regression is that in logistic regression, the output range is bounded between 0 and 1, and a linear relationship between input and output variables is not necessary.

The hypothesis of logistics regression is a sigmoid function. A linear combination of features is taken and a nonlinear sigmoidal function is applied on it.

$$Logistic\ function = \frac{1}{1 + e^{-x}}$$

where x is the input variable. The logistic function is shown in the graph below:

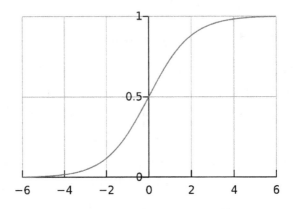

Figure 2: *The Logistic Function [2]*

The logistic function's outcomes are discrete/categorical. Logistic regression uses maximum likelihood estimation (MLE) as a loss function as opposed to linear regression where MSE or RMSE is used as the loss function. MLE is based on conditional probability.

A decision boundary is what helps to classify the data. If you set the decision boundary to 0.5 and use two classes to classify as class-A vs. class-B, when the sigmoid function value is less than 0.5, the output would be class-A and if it is greater than 0.5, it is classified as class-B.

Types of Logistic Regression

There are many types of logistic regression algorithms based on what you are trying to categorize. A binary logistic regression categorizes 2 possible classes. For example, it can be an e-mail categorized as spam or not-spam.

A multi-nominal logistic regression has 3 or more categories without a specific order. An example would be a person's choice of food like vegetarian, non-vegetarian, or vegan.

An ordinal logistic regression has 3 or more categories with ordering. For example, it can be a movie rating of 1, 2, 3, 4, or 5.

Pros and Cons of Logistic Regression

Logistic regression is fast compared to other supervised classification techniques such as SVM or ensemble methods, but it is too simple when you have complex relationships between variables.

Another disadvantage of logistic regression is that it tends to underperform when the decision boundary is nonlinear.

5.4.2 Naïve Bayes Classifier

Naïve Bayes classifier is a probabilistic machine learning model based on Bayes theorem. If you do not remember Bayes theorem, then it is just, "what is the probability that this thing will happen given that the other thing has happened?" You can also think of it as, "what is the probability that this animal is a dog given that it already is a cat?" In this case the probability is 0 unless you are talking about the CatDog animated show. The Bayes theorem is given by the equation:

$$P(A|B) = \frac{P(B|A) \cdot P(A)}{P(B)}$$

where *P(A|B)* is the probability of happening given that *B* has already happened, *P(B|A)* is the opposite of that, and *P(A)*, *P(B)* are probabilities of *A* happening, and *B* happening, respectively.

In the naïve Bayes classifier, we assume that the one particular feature is unaffected by the other predictors/features i.e., features are independent of each other. Naïve Bayes classifier is commonly applied in sentiment analysis, spam filtering, recommendation systems, etc.

Let's use a common dataset to understand this algorithm, the problem of playing golf.

Outlook	Temperature	Humidity	Windy	Play Golf
Rainy	Hot	High	False	No
Rainy	Hot	High	True	No
Overcast	Hot	High	False	Yes
Sunny	Mild	High	False	Yes
Sunny	Cool	Normal	False	Yes
Sunny	Cool	Normal	True	No
Overcast	Cool	Normal	True	Yes
Rainy	Mild	High	False	No
Rainy	Cool	Normal	False	Yes
Sunny	Cool	Normal	False	Yes
Rainy	Cool	Normal	True	Yes

The results of table show that the rainy weather, high temperature, humidity, and zero wind are not suitable conditions for playing golf.

There are two assumptions made here:

1. All the predictors are independent, i.e., high temperature does not necessarily mean high humidity.

2. The outcome is equally affected by all the predictors, i.e., a windy day being windy has no extra importance for playing golf than a hot day.

The variable y is the class variable (play golf), i.e., output. It shows whether the conditions are suitable for playing golf or not. The variable X represents the input parameters/features. Bayes theorem for this problem can be written as follows:

$$P(y|X) = \frac{P(X|y) \cdot P(y)}{P(X)}$$

Here, $X = x_1, x_2, \ldots, x_n$. We can stretch the initial equation as follows:

$$P(y|x_1, \dots, x_n) = \frac{P(x_1|y)P(x_2|y)\dots P(x_n|y)P(y)}{P(x_1)P(x_2)\dots P(x_n)}$$

As you see for all entries in the dataset, the denominator does not change, it remains static. You will notice a proportionality in the equation as follows:

$$P(y|x_1, \dots, x_n) \propto P(y)\Pi_{i=1}^{n}P(x_i|y)$$

If you do not understand this equation, the symbol is the proportionality symbol which states that if one side of the equation increases in value, the other size increases too. Like the air conditioning usage increase is directly proportional to the rising temperature outside. The equation can further be simplified into the following:

$$y = argmax_y P(y)\Pi_{i=1}^{n}P(x_i|y)$$

Why is the *argmax* there? Hint: This is got something to do with an event with a higher probability happening more frequently than one with a lower probability.

Types of Naïve Bayes Classifier

1. **Multinomial Naïve Bayes:** This theorem is mostly used for classification of documents; it helps to find the category of the documents. Whether the document is sports, politics, or technology. The feature/predictor used by this classifier is the frequency of the words that a document contains.

2. **Bernoulli Naïve Bayes:** This is like the multinomial naïve Bayes, but Boolean variables (0/1) are its predictors. The outcomes have only two values yes or no, for example, if a word occurs in the text or not, or whether the game will be played tomorrow or not.

3. **Gaussian Naïve Bayes:** If the predictor's values are not discrete, but instead they are continuous, these values are sampled from

a Gaussian distribution. When the data is Gaussian (normally) distributed, Gaussian naïve Bayes algorithm fits perfect.

Pros and Cons of Naïve Bayes Classifier

A naïve Bayes classifier is easy to build and particularly useful for very large data sets. It is a simple model but it outperforms highly sophisticated classification methods.

The big disadvantage of this classifier is that the predictors should be independent. There are many cases of data in the real world where the predictors are dependent, which can disrupt the performance of the classifier.

5.5 ALGORITHMS FOR BOTH REGRESSION AND CLASSIFICATION

5.5.1 Support Vector Machine (SVM)

The objective of the support vector machine algorithm is to find a hyper-plane in an N-dimensional space that distinctly classifies the data points with the highest margin possible. N is the number of features in your dataset. SVM performs better if you better split the dataset into their respective classes.

What are Hyper-planes?

Hyper-planes are decision boundaries that help classify data points. The number of features determines the dimension of the hyper-plane. For 2 input features, the hyper-plane is just a line. For 3 input features, the hyper-plane becomes a two-dimensional plane.

Data points falling on either side of the hyper-plane can be attributed to different classes. There are many possible hyper-planes that can be selected to separate the two classes of data points.

What are Margins?

Our target is to find a plane with the maximum margin, i.e., it has the maximum distance between data points of both classes. Maximizing the distances between nearest data point (in either class, e.g., green or blue as in the picture below) helps in deciding the right hyper-plane. This distance is called margin. The maximization of the margin distance is helpful for classifying the future data points with more confidence. Another reason for selecting the hyper-plane with a higher margin is robustness. A hyper-plane with a low margin has high chances of misclassification.

What are Support Vectors?

The data points that are closer to the hyper-plane, and hence have the capability of affecting the position and orientation of the hyperplane are called support vectors. Using the support vectors, the margin of the classifier can be maximized. The position of the hyperplane changes by deleting the support vectors. These are the points that help us build our SVM.

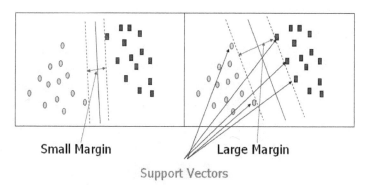

Figure 3: *Support Vectors [3]*

Kernel for Non-Linear Data

When your data is not linear, SVM can solve the problem using a technique called kernel. A function that transforms a low dimensional input space to a higher dimensional space is called an SVM kernel. It basically replaces an inseparable problem with a separable one. It is mostly useful in non-linear separation problem. You can look at how inseparable data points are mapped into a higher dimension to make it separable, and how a hyper-plane is drawn in that dimension in the figure below:

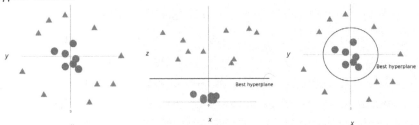

Figure 4: *Higher Dimensional Hyper-plane [4]*

Sigmoid Function

In logistic regression, the output of the linear function is taken and is squeezed within the range [0,1], using the sigmoid function. Label 1 is assigned, if the squeezed value is greater than a threshold value (0.5), otherwise label 0 is assigned. In SVM, if the output is greater than 1, it is identified as one class, but if the output is -1, then it is identified as another class.

Cost Function

The loss function that helps to maximize the margin is called a hinge loss. If the signs of the predicted and actual values are the same, then the cost is 0. If they are the opposite, then we calculate the loss value. We also add a regularization parameter to the cost function. The margin maximization and loss are balanced by the regularization parameter. The cost function, after adding the regularization parameter, becomes:

$$Cost\,function = min_w \lambda |w|^2 + \sum_{i=1}^{n} (1 - y_i \langle w_i, w \rangle)$$

Pros and Cons of Support Vector Machine

SVM works well with a clear margin of separation and is effective in high dimensional spaces. It uses the support vectors that are a subset of training points in the decision function, so it is also memory efficient.

Its disadvantage is that for a large data set, it does not perform well because the required training time is higher. It does not perform well for noisy data either, because the target classes will overlap in noisy datasets.

5.5.2 k-Nearest Neighbors (KNN)

k-nearest neighbors is the algorithm example of, "show me your friends and I will tell you who you are." It assumes that similar things exist in close proximity.

KNN is a lazy learning, non-parametric, and instance-based algorithm. It can be applied easily and can perform very complex classification tasks. It can also solve regression problems.

It is called lazy learning because it makes no generalizations, i.e., no training is required to apply the algorithm. So, when using KNN, all the training data is also used in testing.

It is called a non-parametric learning algorithm because it doesn't assume anything about the underlying data. This is a very important and useful feature of this algorithm because, in real- life, data does not follow any theoretical assumption like linear-separability or uniform distribution, nor do we assume that the structure is simple.

The algorithm is used to find pattern recognition and document similarity widely. It is also an active algorithm for developing recommender systems and for dimensionality reduction and pre-processing steps for computer vision, particularly face recognition tasks.

A visualization of k-NN is shown in the figure below. See how there are 3 clusters, this means the value of k in this example is 3.

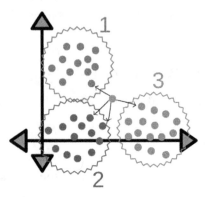

Figure 5: *k-Nearest Neighbors Visualization with k=3 [5]*

Steps for Applying k-NN

1. The distance of a new data point with respect to all other training data points is found.
2. This distance between data points and training points can be Euclidean, Manhattan or any other type.
3. Then the k-nearest data points are selected, where k can be any integer.
4. Finally, k-NN algorithm assigns the data point to the class to which many of the k data points belong.

Euclidean distance is a popular and very familiar choice to find the straight-line distance. It is calculated as shown below:

$$d(p,q) = d(q,p) = \sqrt{\sum_{i=1}^{n}(q_i - p_i)^2}$$

where p, q are the points in space. If you have 2 points in space (like points drawn on your paper), then the Euclidean distance is the length of the line segment you get when you connect the two points together.

Value of k in k-Nearest Neighbors

This is a bit of a trial-and-error method. To select the k that is right for your data, you run the KNN algorithm several times with different values of k and choose the k that reduces the number of errors you encounter, maintaining the algorithm's ability to accurately make predictions when it is given data it has not seen before.

Pros and Cons of k-Nearest Neighbors

KNN is extremely easy to implementand requires no training prior to making real-time predictions. For KNN, there is no need for building models, tuning parameters, or making any assumptions.

One of the disadvantages of using KNN is that it has a high prediction cost for large datasets. Quality of data is highly important; however, it takes a lot of computational power and it may not be a good option if your data volume is huge. It doesn't work well with multi-dimensional data because, as the number of dimensions increases, it becomes difficult for the algorithm to calculate the distance in each dimension.

There is also a requirement for finding an optimal k value (number of nearest neighbors).

5.5.3 Decision Tree

Decision tree is the easiest algorithm to understand in machine learning and there are not many mathematical formulae involved here. It is also referred to as classification and regression trees or CART.

Decision tree represents the whole data in the form of a tree. It navigates through the entire data set while making decisions. It starts with a root node; the decisions are made when it reaches the leaf node or terminal node. The leaf node is the final node of the tree for that branch.

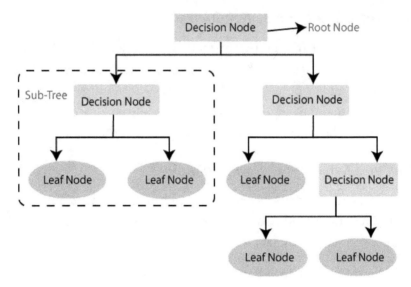

Figure 6: *Decision Tree [6]*

The root of decision trees is at the top, that is, the tree is upside down. The root then splits into several nodes. It is nothing but a group of if-else statements. To give a simple example, if the daylight is sufficient, keep on playing, else stop playing. When the condition mentioned in a node is checked, based on true or false values, the algorithm moves to the left or right of side of the child node.

Terminologies

- Root Node: It is the top node at the beginning of a decision tree. Split starts from this node left to right dividing according to various features.
- Decision Nodes: These come into the picture right after the root, the moment we split the root node.
- Leaf Nodes: These nodes are where further splitting is not possible, they are also called terminal nodes.
- Sub-tree: A sub-section of a decision tree is called sub-tree.

Overfitting

A decision tree can overfit easily even when there is a slight variation in the data. Pruning helps you avoid overfitting the data. Normally, a decision tree makes decisions by looking at the immediate nodes. Considering all the nodes along the chain while making decision process is called pruning.

Let's look at the golf dataset again:

Outlook	Temperature	Humidity	Windy	Play Golf
Rainy	Hot	High	False	No
Rainy	Hot	High	True	No
Overcast	Hot	High	False	Yes
Sunny	Mild	High	False	Yes
Sunny	Cool	Normal	False	Yes
Sunny	Cool	Normal	True	No
Overcast	Cool	Normal	True	Yes
Rainy	Mild	High	False	No
Rainy	Cool	Normal	False	Yes
Sunny	Cool	Normal	False	Yes
Rainy	Cool	Normal	True	Yes

You can create a decision tree for this dataset in the following manner:

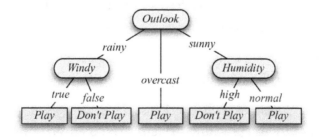

Figure 7: *Decision Tree for Golf Play Dataset [7]*

Greedy in Nature

To create a decision tree, all the features are considered and are split accordingly. Then they are tested using a cost function. The split with the best cost (or lowest cost) is selected. This algorithm is recursive in nature because the groups formed by splitting the features can be sub-divided using the same strategy. Due to this nature, this algorithm is also known as the greedy algorithm, as we have an extreme desire of lowering the cost. So, the root node becomes a best predictor/classifier.

You might be thinking, how do you know what feature is the root node amongst all other features? Well, you will pick the root node feature based on how many data points predicted as expected. This is called the homogeneity principle.

You can imagine a tree growing forever if the dataset has a large number of features, so how do you know when to stop growing the tree? Growing the tree unnecessarily makes your model overfit the dataset. You can control the size of your tree by setting a minimum number of training inputs to use on each leaf, and also by setting the maximum depth of your model. The maximum depth refers to the length of the longest path from a root to a leaf.

Pros and Cons of Decision Trees

Decision trees generate rules readable by humans, interpret and visualize.

They cause errors in classification problems if we have many classes, but the number of training examples are small.

They give strong signs about the most important fields for prediction or classification. Features are selected implicitly.

They can handle both continuous and categorical variables, also non-linear relationships within the data that do not affect the prediction.

One of the only disadvantages of decision trees is that the computational training of these trees is expensive.

5.5.4 Random Forest

Similar to the saying, "trees make up the forest", the decision trees make up the random forest.

Random forest is at the top of the classifier hierarchy compared to other classification algorithms such as logistic regression, support vector machine, naïve Bayes classifier, and decision trees.

Random forest combines multiple decision trees and comes up with the best optimal model. The fundamental concept behind the random forest is a simple but powerful one, "the wisdom of crowds". It works so well because many relatively uncorrelated models (trees) operating as a committee outperform any of the individual constituent models.

The key to this algorithm is low correlation between models – just like how investments with low correlations (like stocks and bonds) come together to form a portfolio that is greater than the sum of its parts. Ensemble predictions are produced in uncorrelated models which are more accurate than any of the individual predictions.

Random Forest is an Ensemble Technique

Ensemble methods combine more than one model to produce the best accuracy. Individual models could be weaker with high bias and high variance. Any model with high bias and high variance is considered a weak model. To combine multiple models, you need to look at each model's outcome and come up with a final decision that is better than the individual models.

In random forest there are two popular ensemble techniques, which are bagging, and boosting.

Bagging

You take a dataset and randomly sample number of samples from it, then train a tree for each sample to give an output, which you then aggregate. This is the process of bagging or bootstrap aggregating. Individual trees are obtained by randomly sampling from the dataset, resulting in different trees. Decision trees are sensitive to the data they are trained on. If the values are changed, even small changes can result in a different tree structure.

Random forest follows the bagging technique to produce the best accuracy. In classification, we will see how a random forest will look like with two trees:

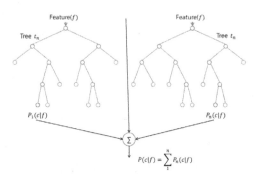

Figure 8: *Bagging Technique for Random Forest [8]*

The hyperparameters in a random forest are nearly the same as in a decision tree or a bagging classifier.

To understand how this works, let's say that you want to spend 1 year vacationing. You decide to take an advice from your close friends. When you ask your best friend, they will advise you according to their own tastes and their past. This is one decision tree. Now you will ask all your other close friends, and finally you have a lot of decision trees. Each friend has their own taste and a unique history of vacations, so in the end you have a random forest with many classifiers from which you will make your final decision.

Boosting

Boosting is another ensemble technique. Here the models are not executed in parallel but are executed in a sequential manner. Model_2 output is dependent on Model_1. The final model (Model_4) is based on the previous models, Model_1, Model_2, and Model_3. Model_2 tries to improve the error rate of Model_1. Similarly, Model_3 tries to improve the error rate of Model_1 and Model_2, and the same is true for Model_4.

Boosting is mainly for custom orchestrations; you can build a super model using boosting and stacking (this involves stacking the models on top of each other). Ada boost and gradient boosting are very popular algorithms.

Pros and Cons of Random Forest

Random forest is versatile. Its default hyperparameters usually produce very good prediction results. There are no overfitting issues in it. If the number of trees in the forest is large, the classifier won't overfit the model.

The disadvantage of random forest is that a large number of trees can slow down the algorithm and make it ineffective for real-time predictions. Random forest is a predictive modelling tool, not a descriptive tool, i.e., you cannot get a description of the relationships in the data.

5.6 SUMMARY

- Supervised learning algorithms can solve regression and classification problems.
- The linear regression algorithm is used for regression problems.
- Naïve Bayes classifier and logistic regression algorithms can be used for classification problems.
- Support vector machine, k-nearest neighbors, decision tree, and random forest algorithms can be used for both classification and regression problems.
- Linear regression is helpful when the input and output have a linear relationship.
- Logistic regression is useful for linearly separable classes.
- Naïve Bayes classifier is important when predictors are

independent of each other, but the outcome is equally affected by all the predictors.

- Support vector machine works well where there is a clear margin of separation, and it is very effective in multi-dimensional space.

- k-NN is easy to implement, and no training is required. It is useful in a low dimensional space and works well given that you choose the right value of k.

- In decision tree, the data is presented in the form of tree. Every branch of the tree separates into 2 parts depending on the if-else output of the branch.

- In random forest, there are several data trees combined to give the best tree.

- Ensemble methods combine more than one model to produce the best accuracy. Predictions produced in an ensemble of uncorrelated models are more accurate than any of the individual model's predictions.

- Each algorithm has its strengths and weaknesses, but these algorithms are very helpful in many problem-solving and decision-making scenarios.

If you made it till here, I highly recommend you continue the learning path by visiting the GitHub repository for this chapter.

https://github.com/a-soundhararajan/machine-learning/tree/main/Supervised

There is also a website (https://letsbecomemlengineers.com) and a YouTube channel for additional content (https://www.youtube.com/channel/UcxxGU_Q6A-8aJlSGP19FYUA).

CHAPTER 6

Unsupervised

Learning by Self

Can I learn without a teacher or guidance? Yes, you can learn by yourself. Babies learn a lot by watching their parents and siblings, even adults watch and mimic people. These are all examples of unsupervised learning. Computers can do the same. In machine learning this is called unsupervised learning.

For unsupervised learning, you want your model to learn by observing the patterns in the data. This type of learning is usually done when there is no target variable (also called labels or output) in the dataset.

6.1 WHY UNSUPERVISED LEARNING?

Yann LeCun, Computer scientist, VP & Chief AI Scientist, Facebook, mentioned this about the true power of unsupervised learning, "if intelligence was a cake, unsupervised learning would be the cake, supervised learning would be the icing on the cake and reinforcement learning would be the cherry on the cake".

It is easier to get unlabeled data from a computer than labeled data. In unsupervised learning, very less effort is required to prepare and audit the training dataset. This is in contrast to the supervised learning where assigning and verification of initial labels require expert human labor.

You can easily see why someone would choose unsupervised learning over supervised learning. Unsupervised learning lets the model find all kinds of unknown patterns in the data. It has the freedom to identify and exploit previously undetected patterns that may not have been noticed by human experts.

With all the advantages of unsupervised learning, there also are some disadvantages that you need to be aware of. One of it being that you cannot get precise information regarding data sorting and the output as the data used in unsupervised learning is unlabeled and not known.

After you finish classifying the data you need to spend time interpreting the results. The classification is also usually less accurate because the input data is not known and not labeled by people in advance. It is also computationally expensive and slow since it deals with a huge amount of data.

6.2 APPLICATIONS OF UNSUPERVISED LEARNING

There are many applications of unsupervised learning because real-world data is not usually labelled. Let us look at some of the applications:

- Customer Market Segmentation: This includes classifying customers by their demographics and shopping preferences, frequency, and the total amount spend. Based on a customer's spending patterns, companies can send targeted promotional offers.

- Recommendation Systems: These are the systems that suggest relevant items to customers. These items can be the content to watch (Netflix / YouTube), news to read (Google/Yahoo

News), products to buy (Amazon eCommerce) or anything else depending on the industry.

- Anomaly Detection: These systems identify the suspicious pattern and notify fraudulent transactions. A bank can use anomaly detection to send you notifications of fraudulent activities.

6.3 TYPES OF UNSUPERVISED LEARNING PROBLEMS

Generally, there are two types of problems that are solved by unsupervised learning. They are clustering and dimensionality reduction. We will learn more about them in the following sections.

6.3.1 Clustering

Clustering, as the name suggests, is the process of clustering similar data points together. Your model needs to take in an unlabeled dataset and find a pattern in order to group similar data points together.

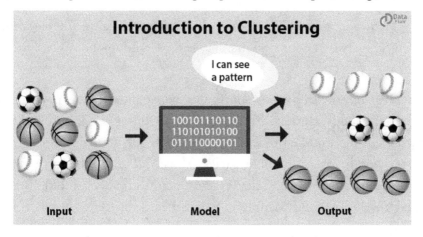

Figure 1: *Clustering [1]*

There are many clustering algorithms used in unsupervised learning. Some common algorithms are k-means clustering, hierarchical clustering, DBSCAN, and mean shift. We will discuss the simplest of these, which is the k-means clustering.

k-means

The process by which observations are divided into k number of clusters is called k-means clustering. The value of k is arbitrary, and finding the perfect k is the most important aspect of k-means clustering. Sometimes it is easy to find the value of k, for example, if you are performing sentiment analysis, then depending on the number of sentiments you want, you will pick the right k (like 2 if you want Positive/Negative sentiments, or 5 if you want Very Positive/Positive/Neutral/Negative/Very Negative). Other times it is much more difficult to assign a definite number for since even you will not know the ideal number of clusters.

Something associated with k is the centroid. A centroid is the imaginary location of the center of the cluster. A point is classified within a cluster depending on the distance between the centroid and the point.

Let's imagine that you have a website and you want to cluster the visitors on your website. You only have 2 datasets, the number of times the visitors visited, and the time of their last visit.

First, you start with the two clusters and initialize the algorithm by picking two random points. These two random points act as the centroids of your clusters.

The second step is to adjust the data points to the new mean/centroid of our clusters. Your target is to bring the centroid (pink square) in the middle of all the pink circles, and similarly blue square in the middle of all the blue circles. Move the centroids, so that they are in the center of the relevant data points (blue vs. pink). Repeat this process until no example is assigned to a different cluster.

The figure below shows the results from the initial cluster assignments.

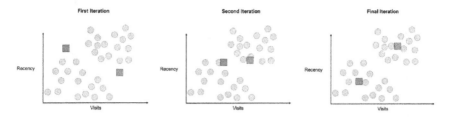

Figure 2: *Steps for Reaching Convergence [2]*

Once the centroids reach the middle of relevant datapoints, don't move them anymore. This is called convergence. By continuously iterating, we are moving to the mean of those identified points that are closest, until they are not able to move anymore. The centroids stay in place, and we have two clusters at this point.

It is actually possible to pick any number of clusters you deem fit. For example, when you choose $k = 3$ you will get clusters like in the figure below:

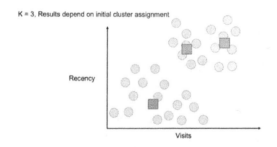

Figure 3: *Cluster Assignments when k=3 [2]*

You will notice that the cluster positions depend on the initial cluster assignments. So, the initial cluster position is important.

Evaluating Cluster Performance

After you have created a lot of clusters, the natural next question is about the evaluation of the clusters. One way to do this is by using inertia.

The inertia gives you the total sum of squared distance of each point to its cluster centroid. Inertia is a popular metric to understand the entropy built into the different clusters. One drawback of using inertia is that this value will be sensitive to the number of points in the clusters. The initial inertia changes if we keep on adding more points. It will not matter that those points are relatively closer to the centroid than the existing points.

The second method is called distortion. Distortion takes the average of the squared distances from each point to its cluster centroid. It does not necessarily increase on adding more points because the closer points will be helpful in decreasing the average distance.

Inertia and distortion both are the measures of entropy per cluster.

Inertia always increases as more points are added to each cluster. But distortion is not affected much as it works by taking the average. Thus,

- Inertia is used where clusters have similar numbers of points.
- Distortion is used where similarity of points in the cluster is more important.

Which Model Is the Right One?

When you are using k-means to cluster, you should initiate the model multiple times and take the model with the best score. With different initial configurations and different k values chosen, you can compute the resulting inertia or distortion. In the end, you will know which model is the best by comparing the inertia or distortion of the models.

So, the next question is, how should you use inertia or distortion to find the right number of clusters? The nature of inertia and distortion is that they both almost always decrease when the number of clusters increase. There is a way to choose the ideal number of clusters using inertia and distortion, and it is called the elbow method. In this method, the number of clusters (k) are varied from 1 to 10, and the inertia and distortion are calculated for each value of k.

The figure below contains graphs with the number of clusters on the x-axis and either inertia or distortion on that y-axis. We can see that, until the inflection point, the inertia or distortion goes down very rapidly. But after the inflection point, the decreasing rate slows down quite dramatically.

This slowing down gives a natural point of our data set where the number of groupings makes sense and should be the logical value of k. Based on this diagram, optimal k value would be "3", which falls right at the elbow section.

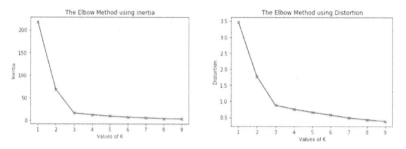

Figure 4: *The Elbow Method [3]*

The problem with the k-means algorithm is that the performance of the model depends on the value of k, and it is also very sensitive to the value of k. Changing the k value gives a different result. So, the cluster will look different every time you run the k-means algorithm.

6.3.2 Dimensionality Reduction

Dimensionality reduction uses the structural characteristics to simplify the data without losing much information from the original data set.

For example, if you want to transform a high-resolution image into an image with a lower resolution, you would not want to lose any detail on the image. The images should look alike, and the method to do that effectively is called the dimensionality reduction method.

Performing dimensionality reduction speeds up the training and improves the performance in some cases. It is extremely useful in data visualization by reducing the multi-dimensions to two or three dimensions to plot a condensed view so as to understand important insights by visually looking at the patterns.

Intuitive Understanding of Dimensionality Reduction

Human beings prefer things that are simple, and straightforward in many cases. When humans first see the color magenta, we think of it as a purplish red sort of thing, where two colors are actually mixed together. After a while, you become familiar and comfortable referring to the color as magenta. You then feel that calling the color magenta is so much better than calling it purplish red, and hence you start identifying it as magenta. You essentially reduced the color from two recognizable variables to one recognizable variable. You performed dimensionality reduction in your brain.

Curse of Dimensionality

In theory, increasing the features improves the performance. Models have more things to learn from, but in practice, too many features lead to a worse performance. Some of those features could be correlated in a spurious manner, meaning they correlate within your dataset, but maybe they do not correlate outside your dataset as new data comes in. A large number of features result in more noise and less useful signals.

Most importantly, the performance of a model slows down as the number of dimensions increases because, in this case, the algorithm has to deal with more columns which are computationally more expensive.

There are a lot of algorithms that perform dimensionality reduction, some of which are principal component analysis (PCA), random projections, Isomap, and t-distributed stochastic neighbor embedding (t-SNE).

Let us take a look at PCA as it is the most widely used dimensionality reduction algorithm.

Principal Component Analysis (PCA)

When you are performing PCA, you are basically creating a new coordinate system and inputting points from the original data. You will project the original data, and the point with the greatest variance will be plotted on the first coordinate. Then the second highest variance will be plotted on the second coordinate and so on.

A low-dimensional representation of the dataset can be obtained using PCA. This representation can have as many variations as possible. Therefore, we only get the most interesting features because they are responsible for most of the variance.

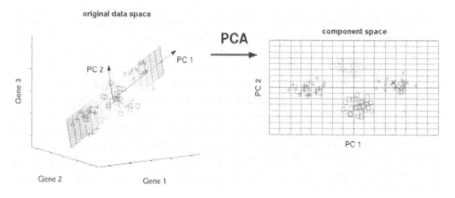

Figure 5: *Translation and Rotation of axes in PCA [4]*

6.4 SUMMARY

- Real-world datasets do not have everything labeled. Hence, unsupervised learning is one of the most important concepts in machine learning.
- Clustering and dimensionality reduction are the common applications of unsupervised learning.
- k-means is a type of clustering algorithm in which k number of clusters are created on an unlabeled data. The number of clusters can be chosen by inertia or distortion.
- Principal component analysis is an algorithm used for dimensionality reduction. It reduces the dimensions of the data by choosing axes where the variance of the data is the highest, and moving on to the second highest variance and so on. There will be as many principal components as there are variables in the data.

Now that you have reached the end of the chapter, I highly recommend you continue the learning path by visiting the GitHub repository for this chapter.

https://github.com/a-soundhararajan/machine-learning/tree/main/Unsupervised

There is also a website (https://letsbecomemlengineers.com/) and a YouTube channel (https://www.youtube.com/channel/UCxxGU_Q6A-8aJlSGP19FYUA) with additional content.

CHAPTER 7

Deep Learning

Artificial Neural Networks

Have you ever wondered how mundane the act of driving is? Or maybe you have wondered if you could have a personal assistant who can give you weather updates, play your favorite music, and order a pizza without paying them money. Well, deep learning is your answer. Deep learning is everywhere, and it is present in many places in our daily life in the form of smartphone apps and voice assistant devices like Alexa, and Google Home.

Alexa played a critical role in my life during the COVID-19 pandemic. Those of us with kids found it incredibly hard to maintain a work-life balance. I give Alexa the full credit for helping my 6-year-old daughter with her remote learning. Alexa reminds my daughter of her breaks, Zoom sessions, etc. That way I was able to focus on my work.

Machine learning is already a powerful statistical model, but the disadvantage of statistical implementation is that human intervention in feature selection is unavoidable. Usually, these human interventions can only be done by experts in a particular field where machine learning is employed.

Deep learning is a type of machine learning as depicted in Figure 1. It is very different compared to the machine learning statistical models. Deep learning includes artificial neural networks (ANN), and these days the two terms are used somewhat interchangeably.

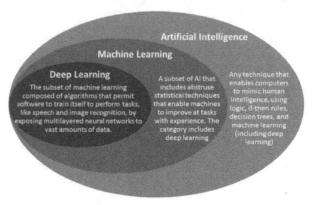

Figure 1: *Field of Artificial Intelligence. [1]*

7.1 HARDWARE FOR DEEP LEARNING

Deep learning, as we will see further along in the chapter, requires a lot of calculations. To perform these calculations in as short a time span as possible, we require processors called Graphical Processing Units (GPUs) which excel in multiprocessing. GPUs are more than 70 times faster than CPUs, which in turn decreases the training time for neural networks. Smaller neural networks can train in a few minutes, while large neural networks will take hours or even a few days to get trained.

You might be thinking, what makes GPUs so much better than CPUs in parallel calculations? The answer is its parallel processing capability. GPUs like NVIDIA A100 has 6912 CUDA cores. Hence, the calculation requirements of neural networks, which includes matrix and vector calculations that are required for the backpropagation technique, are accelerated when performed in GPUs. The backpropagation technique is about adjusting weights and biases in a neural network to lower the cost function. Given the advancement of cloud technologies, GPUs are easily available to everyone today.

7.2 DATA

Recent digital transformation and growth of data pushed the deep learning from research labs to real life applications, but the fundamental algorithms have been there for the last 20 years. According to a Forbes article in May 2018, a total of 2.5 quintillion bytes of data is being generated every day from billions of internet-connected devices.

Deep learning requires a lot of data to perform better. It can solve complex problems, and the way it can solve them is by processing large amounts of data and looking for patterns to discover a way to calculate the output. Unless you have a lot of data, it is not recommended to train neural networks. You should begin by solving your problem using a rule-based heuristic approach or statistical machine learning methods and move on to deep learning when you hit the limit on these traditional approaches.

7.3 NEURAL NETWORKS

It is a popular myth that computers and human beings learn in a similar fashion but that is false. Repetition and revision are the foundations of human learning. Machine learning and deep learning are all fancy math and pattern matching, which is a completely different way of information processing when compared to that done by the human mind.

Neural networks are the foundation of deep learning wherein data is processed through computing units called neurons. Neurons are arranged in hierarchically ordered layers. The order of neurons is up to the architect of the neural network. This is why neural networks are highly flexible and can solve many complex problems like image recognition, speech recognition, and natural language processing.

One of the main differences between machine learning and deep learning comes from feature selection. Machine learning requires human intervention to define the correct features that will give the best performance while deep learning does not require human intervention for feature selection. The layers of a neural network are capable of identifying their own features.

The concept of neural network is based on the functioning of a human brain, but no computer can exactly model the functions of a human brain like reasoning, problem solving and learning. Therefore, the neural networks created by humans are called artificial neural networks.

504192

Figure 2: *Handwritten Digits from MNIST Dataset [2]*

If you look at Figure 2, you can easily recognize the handwritten digits as 504192. In each hemisphere of your brain, you have a primary visual cortex (V1) that contains millions of neurons. When you see an image like the one above, the human vision not only involves V1, but an entire series of visual cortices (V2, V3, V4, and V5) which progressively do more complex image processing. When it comes to machines, recognizing handwritten digits is not that easy for them.

7.4 PERCEPTRON

Before we discuss ANN and its architecture further, let us understand the history of neural networks and neural networks in their most basic form.

The simplest form of a neural network is known as the perceptron. The perceptron was developed during the 1950s and 1960s by a scientist named Frank Rosenblatt, inspired by earlier works of McCulloch and Walter Pitts.

A perceptron takes inputs like x_1, x_2, ...x_n that are all binary, and produces a single binary output:

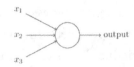

Figure 3: *Perceptron [3]*

In the examples shown in Figure 3, the perceptron has 3 inputs, x_1, x_2, x_3. It has a simple rule to compute the output which includes weights, w_1, w_2, w_3. A weight is a real number that expresses how important an input is to the output. The neurons binary output (0/1) is determined by whether the weighted sum is greater or lower than a threshold value. The threshold value is a real number and is considered the parameter of the neuron. A neuron's output is calculated as below:

$$output = \begin{cases} 0; \; if \sum_j w_j x_j \leq threshold \\ 1; \; if \sum_j w_j x_j > threshold \end{cases}$$

The perceptron also has another parameter which can be tuned. This is called a bias. You can think of a bias as how easy is it for a perceptron to give an output of 1. If a perceptron has a large value of bias, then it is easy for it to give an output of 1.

Hence, the equation becomes like this:

$$output = \begin{cases} 0; \; if \; w.x + b \leq 0 \\ 1; \; if \; w.x + b > 0 \end{cases}$$

This is how a perceptron functions, but the disadvantage of a perceptron is that a small change in bias or weight is enough to flip the output of the perceptron. To solve this problem, you will require the sigmoid activation function.

7.4.1 Perceptron with Activation Functions

Activation functions are mathematical functions which define the output of a node. In the case of perceptron, we will be using a sigmoid function. The sigmoid function is mathematically defined as:

$$\sigma(x) = \frac{1}{1 + e^{-\sum_j w_j x_j - b}}$$

The graph of the sigmoid function looks like this:

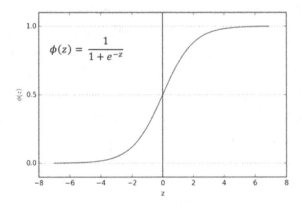

Figure 4: *Graph of a Sigmoid Function [4]*

The sigmoid function makes the output of the perceptron to be any value between 0 and 1. Thus, a small change in weights does not change the output of the perceptron as drastically as before.

7.5 ARTIFICIAL NEURAL NETWORK

In a basic ANN, the leftmost layer is the input layer, and the rightmost layer is the output layer. All the middle layers are called the hidden layers.

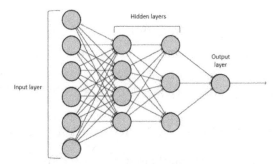

Figure 5: *Artificial Neural Network [5]*

7.5.1 Input and Output Layers

The easiest part of designing a neural network is designing the input and output layers. The input layer should correspond to the shape of the input tensor, and the output layer should correspond to the target vectors you have (if your learning is supervised).

For example, if you want to create a model that recognizes handwritten digits, then the input can be a 64 × 64 grayscale image. The image will need a total of 64 × 64 = 4096 input neurons, with intensity scaled between 0 and 1. The output layer will contain 10 neurons, which correspond to the numbers 0-to-9.

7.5.2 Hidden Layers

Designing the hidden layers is an art that has no simple rules. Researchers have developed many design recommendations for hidden layers which you can use as a guidance, but you can also go ahead and design the hidden layers your own way.

There are some quick things that you should know about the design of the hidden layers. Firstly, the number of hidden layers you should have depends on the complexity of the problem you are solving. The amount of training time you spend is directly proportional to the number of these hidden layers in your network. Generally, the more hidden layers you have, the better the performance of your neural network.

7.5.3 Activation Functions

As explained before, an activation function is a non-linear function which helps the neural network generalize a non-linear problem. This activation function controls the final output of a node and passes it as the input to the next layer of the neural network. An activation function is non-linear and hence, not a straight line.

There are various activation functions, each suited for a different application. Some of them are listed below:

- Step Function: This function has a real threshold value, and it gives an output of 1 if the input is greater than the chosen threshold, and gives an output of 0 if the input is lower than the chosen threshold. Step function is not a good activation function as it doesn't fit all the real-world non-linear data scenarios, and it can only be used if you have 2 classes.

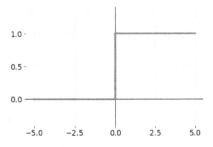

Figure 6: *Graph of a Step Function [6]*

- Linear Function: A linear function is given by the equation, *y* = *mx* + *c*, which you may know as the equation of a straight line. This function gives an output in the form of an analog value, so the network only activates one class. This is useful when there is a possibility of more than one class neuron getting fired. One downfall of this function is that is derivative and it is a constant.

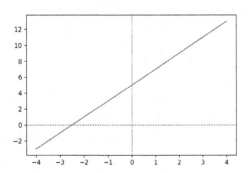

Figure 7: *Graph of a Linear Function [7]*

- Sigmoid Function: This is a non-linear function, and the layers can be stacked if this function is used. This gives an output in the form of an analog value, and it is widely used in the output layer of classification neurons. One disadvantage of this function is that it has a vanishing gradient problem.

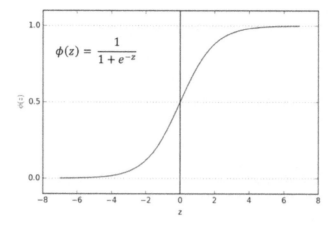

Figure 4: *Graph of a Sigmoid Function [4]*

- Tanh Function: This function is very similar to the sigmoid function. It is non-linear, and the layers can be stacked. It has a steeper derivative than the sigmoid function. It also has a vanishing gradient problem.

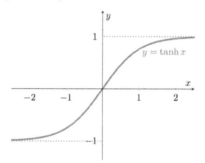

Figure 8: *Graph of a Tanh Function [8]*

- ReLU Function: The Rectified Linear Unit function gives an output of 0 when the input is less than the threshold value, and emits the input value as output when the input is above the threshold value. Generally, the default threshold value is 0. ReLU does not activate all neurons at the same time. Hence, this function is computationally cheap. This function solves the vanishing gradient problem. It learns faster and performs better than linear and sigmoid functions. If you do not know what activation function to use, you can use the ReLU function.

ReLU has shown significant increases in prediction accuracies when compared to other functions. One of its problems is that the gradient becomes 0 along the way in the network. This is called the dying ReLU problem.

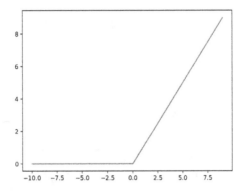

Figure 9: *Graph of ReLU Function [9]*

- Leaky ReLU Function: Leaky Rectified Linear Unit is a variation to the original ReLU function, and it is the solution for the dying ReLU problem. It makes the horizontal line into a non-horizontal line as shown below. This ensures that the gradient is never 0.

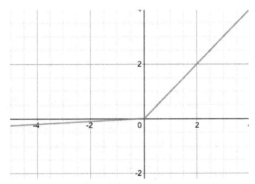

Figure 10: *Graph of Leaky ReLU [10]*

7.5.4 What Activation Function Should I Use?

Each layer of neural networks can be designed with a different activation function. It has been the trend in current years to use the ReLU activation function in the hidden layers of the network. ReLU performs better than all other activation function and it is computationally cheap, so it is a win-win situation.

When it comes to the activation functions to be used in the output layer, it depends. If you have a binary classification problem, then you need to use the sigmoid function. But if you have a multi-class classification problem, you need to use the Log-Softmax function.

In the end, the type of activation function you need to use requires a little bit of research, and a bit of trial-and-error.

7.6 HOW DOES AN ANN LEARN?

The basic form of a neural network is known as artificial neural network (ANN). We will investigate how a neural network works step-by-step. To give you an overview, the neural network performs a forward-pass to get an output from the network. Then the output of the network is compared with the known outputs, and a loss is calculated (cost function). The loss value is used in the backpropagation step to change the weights and biases of the model to reduce the loss value, and make the model perform better. Then the cycle restarts from the first step all over again.

7.6.1 Forward Propagation

To understand how a neural network forward propagates, you need to know what a neural network consists of. The most fundamental element of a neural network is a node.

A node in a neural network is exactly like the perceptron you learnt about earlier in this chapter. It takes an input and gives an output, but in this case the output is usually the input for the next layer of the neural network. If you see any diagram of a neural network (for example, Figure 7.5 above), the circles are the nodes.

Forward propagation of a neural network happens when the input layer takes in an input vector and this input vector calculates its output vector. Then the first hidden layer takes those inputs and continues to process through the subsequent hidden layers. Eventually, the output of the hidden layers will reach the output layer as its input, and the output layer will give an outcome, which will be the final output of the whole network. This output can now be compared to the expected output to calculate the cost function (if you are doing supervised learning).

7.6.2 Cost Function

A neural network needs the optimal weights in its layers to give the right output for a certain input. To do this, we need an algorithm that lets us find how similar the predicted output is to the real output. This is done by the cost function. A cost function is defined as follows:

$$C(w, b) \equiv \frac{1}{2n} \sum_x |y(x) - a|^2$$

This cost function (denoted by C) is a quadratic function, and it is popularly known as the mean squared error (MSE). The output of the cost function is always non-negative. As the output of the cost function becomes smaller, the output $y(x)$ gets closer to the real output. Hence, as long as the value of the cost function decreases after every iteration, the neural network is learning in the positive direction.

The aim of our training algorithm is to minimize the cost function. The output is very accurate if $C(w, b) \approx 0$. So, the next task is to find a way to use the information of the cost function and improve the accuracy of the neural network model. The way to achieve this is by using a gradient descent.

7.6.3 Backpropagation

In backpropagation, the information is passed from the output layers to the input layers. Backpropagation is the main reason why the performance of neural networks is better than statistical machine learning methods.

In our exploration, we have already calculated the loss of the model. Now, it is time to use the loss to fine tune the network by changing the weights and biases of the network.

To change the weight, we need to know how much the particular weight affects the error of the network. This is done by the following equation:

$$W_x = W_x - \eta \frac{\delta Error}{\delta W_x}$$

This equation shows how a weight in x-th layer of a network is changed based on the error calculated and the learning rate set by you.

After all the weights are changed for a particular iteration, the new network commences again with the forward propagation. What happens is that these small changes make the network more accurate after each iteration. Eventually, the cost value will be almost zero, and the final predicted output will match the real output.

7.6.4 Summary of How an ANN Learns

Let's recap the steps of making the neural network learn. The first thing that happens in the network is to initialize the parameters (weights, biases) of the network with random values. Thereafter, you will input the vectors that are already processed to fit in the network without any errors.

After you input the vectors into the model, they will pass through the whole network and give you an output using a process called forward propagation. This output is called the predicted output (predicted by the model without any outside intervention). The predicted output is then compared with the correct output (if the learning is supervised), and a special function called a loss function (or cost function) is used to find out how wrong the predicted output is compared to the actual output. The best possible outcome for any model is for the loss function be the lowest possible, so an optimization algorithm is used to minimize the values of the loss function.

A special process called backpropagation is used to propagate the loss back through the network. In this process, the weights are changed a little bit so that the overall performance of the model increases.

All these steps are performed many times. In the field of deep learning, an epoch corresponds to a single cycle of training the network with all the training data. So, depending on the type of network and the performance in its first epoch, you need to decide how many epochs the network needs before it reaches its best possible performs (this again is trial-and-error).

7.7 OPTIMIZATION ALGORITHMS

To understand all the optimization algorithms, let us start with the one where it all began, the gradient descent algorithm.

7.7.1 Gradient Descent (GD)

The gradient descent algorithm is an optimization algorithm which is used to find the minimum of a given function. Now what is the function that we would love to minimize? It is the cost function, so the gradient descent algorithm works by repeatedly computing the gradient of the cost function and eventually reaching the minimum value of the cost function. The gradient vector of the cost function is given by the equation:

$$\nabla C \equiv \left(\frac{\delta C}{\delta v_1}, \frac{\delta C}{\delta v_2} \right)^T$$

The change in parameter is done as shown in the equation below:

$$\Delta v = -\eta \nabla C$$

Where η is the learning rate of the neural network which you yourself set.

To show how a gradient descent algorithm works, we will look at the figure given below:

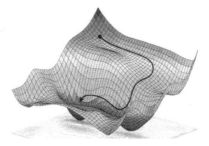

Figure 11: *How Does a Gradient Descent Algorithm Work? [11]*

Imagine this hilly terrain is a plotted graph of the cost function which you are trying to minimize. Let us look at how it works:

- The gradient descent algorithm picks a random point in the graph (which is shown by the black dot in the graph).
- Then the algorithm calculates the gradient of the point it is on.
- Then it takes a short step to the lowest negative gradient (a.k.a. the steepest slope of the hill).
- Then the steepest slope point becomes the new starting point, after which it performs the above steps again. This will eventually lead to the lowest point in the graph (as can be seen in the graph).

Remember that in the 3rd step we took a small step in the most negative direction? This short step is the parameter of the learning rate that you set. There is a chance that the graph looks like this:

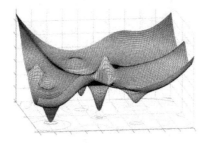

Figure 12: *Gradient Descent with Local Minima [12]*

Do you notice how there are a lot of minimum points on this particular graph (those minimum points are called local minima)? How will you know if your cost function has this type of a graph or a graph with only one minimum? The truth is that we do not know, so the learning rate we set needs to compensate for the fact that we do not have this information.

Having a high learning rate makes the algorithm never reach a minimum point and having a very low learning rate also makes the algorithm never reach the minimum point. Having an unsuitable learning rate gets the algorithm stuck in the local minima and it never reach the global minima. How do we find the best learning rate? Nobody can give you the correct answer, you have to perform a trial-and-error search to find the perfect learning rate for you.

7.7.2 Stochastic Gradient Descent (SGD)

Stochastic gradient descent is an improvement on the traditional gradient descent method. What it does is that it takes a subset of training examples rather than the whole training batch. SGD converges much faster compared to the gradient descent algorithm.

7.7.3 Other Optimizers

There are a lot of other optimizers that you can use in your network. SGD and GD are only two of the choices. Here are some of the different optimizers you can use:

- Adaptive Gradient Algorithm (AdaGrad): AdaGrad is a type of optimizer that adapts its learning rate based on the parameters by incorporating the knowledge of the past observations. This improves the performance on problems with sparse gradients (sparse gradients give you the vanishing gradient problem, meaning the backpropagation cannot tune the weights. It can be seen in NLP, and computer vision).

- Root Mean Squared Propagation (RMSprop): Root Mean Squared Propagation is an optimizer which is a mix of the AdaGrad and SGD. It maintains a per-parameter learning rate based on the recent gradients calculated. This algorithm performs well with online tasks and noisy data.

- Adam: The Adam optimizer takes the advantages of both the RMSprop and the AdaGrad. Adam can handle both sparse gradients as well as noisy data.

7.7.4 What Optimizer Should I Use?

You might have a question in your mind as to which optimization algorithm from among gradient descent, stochastic gradient descent, AdaGrad, RMSprop, and Adam should you use.

You should use Adam. It is suggested that Adam be kept as the default optimization method for all deep learning applications. It performs better than all other optimization algorithms.

Now that we know about gradients, we will look into the vanishing gradient problem.

7.7.5 The Vanishing Gradient Problem

The vanishing gradient problem is a big problem in the deep learning space. When you use a gradient optimizing algorithm in a neural network, it calculates the gradient per node of the network. This gradient is used to change the value of the weight. Sometimes when you calculate the gradient, you get a very small value and the weights do not get updated as you hope for. When this happens, the network will completely stop learning. As you can imagine, this can happen more and more frequently if you have a larger number of layers.

There are various ways to keep your network from suffering from the vanishing gradient problem. One of the ways is to change the activation functions in the network. ReLU has a lower probability of the vanishing gradient problem and can be used to address this issue. Another way is to use alternate weight initialization schemes, such as He initialization and Xavier initialization methods which are outside the scope of this book.

7.8 HOW TO MAKE MY NEURAL NETWORK LEARN MORE?

There will come a point where your neural network will stop learning no matter how much data you feed into it. Usually, you need to stop your neural network's learning process before you reach this point (which is a completely different topic that we will not cover in this book, look-up the concept called "early stopping to avoid overtraining neural networks" of further reading) but there are a few methods which can improve your networks.

7.8.1 More Edge Cases

Generally, when you have a lot of data to train a neural network, you tend to have a lot of similar kind of data but not enough data to cover all the edge case scenarios.

This can be seen in self-driving cars' data. For example, there is billions of hours of footage of a car just driving down a lane, but there are little data on a car stopping because a dog ran in front of it. You can create a good self-driving AI which can stay keep a car in a lane, but that AI might not brake when a dog comes in front of your car.

Now, it will be your job as the creator of the self-driving car's AI to find as much data for edge cases as possible and feed it into your model so that the AI will be experienced in everything in addition to driving down a lane.

7.8.2 Transfer Learning

Transfer learning happens when you use a neural network which has already been trained by someone else on your data. In this scenario, you do not need to start from scratch when you train the neural network.

There are a lot of networks like BERT, ViT, etc. which are pre-trained, and you can further train them yourself for your own cases.

7.8.3 Hidden Layers

Hidden layers are all the layers which are not the input and output layers. There are research papers that conclude that the performance of the neural network model increases as you add more layers to it. You can use this to your advantage by pushing your network to its limit. Although the more layers you add, the slower the whole neural network becomes in training and calculating the output.

7.9 SUMMARY

- Deep learning is a category of machine learning.
- It does not require you to be a domain expert in the field you are tackling, unlike statistical methods where you need human experts for feature selections.
- Neural networks are simple mathematical models that compute the output from an input by applying mathematical functions.
- They have a lot of layers made up of nodes which calculate an output, each node will have an activation function that changes the output into something that can easily be the input of the next layer.
- A neural network's performance is directly proportional to the number of hidden layers in it. When you add more than necessary hidden layers, the training becomes slow.
- Neural networks use optimization algorithms to change the weights and biases of each node to make it learn how to perform a particular function.
- Gradient descent, stochastic gradient descent, AdaGrad, RMSprop, and Adam are popular optimization algorithms. Adam is kept as the default optimization algorithm for most deep learning solutions.

Now that you have reached the end of the chapter, I highly recommend you continue the learning path by visiting the GitHub repository for this chapter.

https://github.com/a-soundhararajan/machine-learning/tree/main/DeepLearning-ANN

There is also a website (https://letsbecomemlengineers.com/) and a YouTube channel (https://www.youtube.com/channel/UCxxGU_Q6A-8aJlSGP19FYUA) with additional content.

CHAPTER 8

Special Networks

RNN & CNN

In this chapter we will investigate the different types of neural networks. The artificial neural network (ANN) that you read about in the previous chapter is the basic form of neural networks. In general, there are 3 types of neural networks:

- Artificial Neural Network (ANN)
- Recurrent Neural Network (RNN)
- Convolutional Neural Network (CNN)

We will first look into the recurrent neural networks, and then the convolutional neural networks.

8.1 RECURRENT NEURAL NETWORK

Recurrent neural networks are a special type of neural networks that can handle sequential or time-series data. This type of data can be anything that changes its value based on time, or you can say that when time flows, the data changes. Data from sensors, stock market prices, communication signals, and voice commands fall under time-series signals. All of these can be processed very well by the recurrent neural networks.

If you interpret a voice sample content, each word comes after the previous one, and this goes on and on. A voice sample falls under sequential data, and the reason we specify sequential OR time-series is because some data are just sequential but not time-series. Data like natural language are sequential (you can see one word coming after the other in this book), but words are not time-series. So, we can come to a conclusion that the recurrent neural networks are very good at processing data that comes one after the other and using the positions of the data point to create a model.

8.1.1 Architecture of RNN

Now, let's see what an RNN looks like.

Feed forward networks have an input layer, a hidden layer, and an output layer. When you look further at the feed-forward network (ANN), the network does not remember anything and it does not have a memory of the data that went through it in the previous nodes. Also, the input vector size is fixed. What if you want your network to remember the previous inputs because you know that it will help the network perform better? Or what if you want the network to accept any size of input? In such cases, RNN is the solution for you.

RNNs have an internal memory state that stores the previous input state. This is done through a feedback loop attached to it, as can be seen in the figure below.

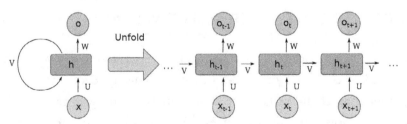

Figure 1: *Recurrent Neural Network Showing Feedback Loop [1]*

8.1.2 Issues with Recurrent Neural Networks

RNNs suffer from the well-known vanishing gradient problem. The gradients carry the information for updating the parameters of RNN, but when the gradients become too small to make any difference, the learning stops. This especially happens in case of long sequences of input data. This is called the short-term memory issue. The RNN learns through the previous state information, but it cannot retain the previous information for a long period of time, it will ultimately be lost.

So, RNNs are good at processing sequential data but not very long sequential data. What do you in this case? Well, you build a new type of recurrent neural network. That is exactly what was done, and a new network called Long Short-Term Memory (LSTM) was created.

8.1.3 Long Short-Term Memory

LSTM networks are a special type of RNN. LSTM is good at handling very long sequences of data because its architecture is slightly different compared to that of RNN's.

Now you might be thinking, what makes LSTM special? The answer is its cell state (as shown in Figure 2):

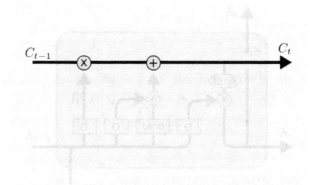

Figure 2: *Cell State of Long Short-Term Memory [2]*

This cell state runs through the LSTM and its "gates" make some minor modifications to it. In a perfect scenario, this cell state will remember all the right things it came across in the previous thousands of data points. To give you an example, if you feed a book chapter containing10 pages about a person named Adam to the LSTM, the cell state should ideally remember that Adam is a male, or that he is an engineer.

We came across "gates", now we should look into what those are. Gates in LSTM are special structures that let some information through. LSTM has 3 gates – the input gate, the output gate, and the forget gate. The input gate looks at the input data and decides what information is fit to be stored in the cell, the output gate gives out a filtered cell state, and the forget gate decides what old information is fit to be forgotten.

The LSTM looks like the following figure.

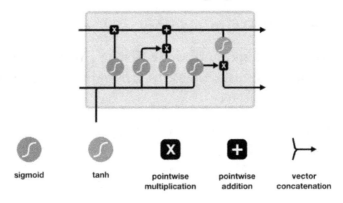

Figure 3: *Long Short-Term Memory [3]*

You might notice that the LSTM is very complicated given it has 3 gates to process the sequential data. Well, there is a version of LSTM that is simpler and performs just as well. It is called the gated recurrent unit.

8.1.4 Gated Recurrent Unit (GRU)

Gated recurrent units combine the forget and input gates of the LSTM into a single gate called the update gate. The cell state and the hidden state (short term memory state) is also merged. In the end, the model of GRU is much simpler compared to that of the LSTM.

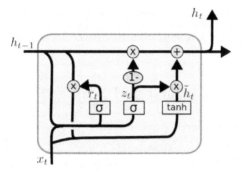

Figure 4: *Gated Recurrent Unit [4]*

Now that we have learned about recurrent neural networks, we will look into another type of network called convolutional neural networks.

8.2 CONVOLUTIONAL NEURAL NETWORK

Convolutional neural network is also known as ConvNet. This type of network is prominently used in computer vision tasks. This is fitting since this network was inspired from the visual cortex of the animal brain.

CNNs work well with complex unstructured data like images, audios, and videos. If a task requires you to use your eyes, you can bet that a CNN will be good at performing that task. It can process images to spot certain objects in images, detect cancer, and identify images to classify them. It can process videos to help you in self-driving, aid in surveillance, detect faces in videos, and a lot more.

8.2.1 Background

In the past, it was a struggle to design a system that can understand visual data. The field of understanding visual data is called computer vision. It aims at enabling machines to view the world as humans do.

CNN was first developed in the 1980s. Much like all deep learning models, it requires a lot of data to train correctly and perform well, and this was a major challenge for using CNNs back in the day. It failed to enter the mainstream world.

Since the 1980s there has been a huge leap in the performance of CNN owing to the endless number of researchers working on computer vision.

8.2.2 Why CNNs over Feed-Forward Neural Networks?

You might be thinking, images are just rows and columns of pixel values. Why do we not just flatten the matrix of an image and pass it into a feed-forward network to classify it? This can work, believe it or not, but it does not work for complicated images. For complicated images you need to use CNNs.

The second disadvantage of using a feed-forward neural network for images is that it grows along with the size of the input image, which might lead it to have tens of thousands of nodes in the input layer. This is not a problem in CNN because you just need to have a constant number of channels for the input, and a size for the filter which we will learn about further ahead.

CNNs are created to work well in capturing the spatial and temporal dependencies in an image through the application of relevant filters. You might be thinking to yourself, what are these filters? Well, a filter in a CNN is a hyperparameter that you have to pick for your model.

A CNN works by taking a window of values from a matrix of vectors and convoluting it with a kernel filter like this:

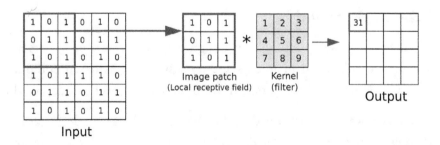

Figure 5: *Working of a Convolutional Neural Network [5]*

That * sign is the symbol for convolution. If you know what a convolution is, that's great, but you do not need to know how it is used in signals and systems to understand how it is used in neural networks. In neural networks, it is like finding the dot product of flattened matrices (or you just multiply each number with the corresponding number of the other matrix and add everything together).

If you look at the image above and imagine a 3 × 3 window forming in the rest of the input, you will see how the CNN can capture the spatial and temporal dependencies. This is just the beginning of how a CNN works, we will now look into the big picture of how a CNN performs computer vision tasks.

8.2.3 CNN Architecture

The neural network model utilizing the convolutional neural network can have 3 different layers that work well together. They are:

1. Convolutional Layer
2. Pooling Layer
3. Fully Connected Layer

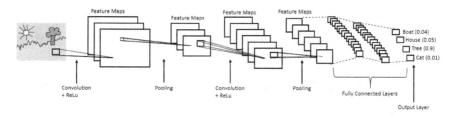

Figure 6: *Convolutional Neural Network Architecture [6]*

Let's build a roadmap to see how these 3 layers come together.

1. You will provide an image input to the convolution layer. When designing the convolutional layer you will choose the filter, stride, and padding for the layer. Then this layer will perform the convolution on the input image and give an output through the ReLU activation function.

2. The pooling layer gives the maximum vector in a kernel as the output. This also has a positive side-effect of reducing the dimensionality of the vector. When designing the pooling layer, you will choose the kernel size, and padding.

3. You can have many convolutional layers and pooling layers one after the other. It is up to you to choose the right number of layers (it is a bit of a trial-and-error method).

4. Finally, when you finish with the nth pooling layer, you need to feed the matrix into a fully connected (FC) layer . You will pick the correct activation function according to the task you are performing (for example, use the log-softmax function if you are classifying images into more than 2 classes), and you will get the output.

Let us investigate each step in further detail.

Convolutional Layer

This is the first layer that extracts the features from the input image. As already stated above, this layer will preserve the spatial relationships of the input matrix. You need to pick some hyperparameters for this layer, they are:

- Filter Size: This is the window size that we looked at before. In the first try, keep it as 3 × 3 and you can change it later if this does not work.

- Stride: This is how much each window will jump, so if you pick 1, then the window will jump only 1 pixel to the right each time. If you pick 2, then the window will jump past 2 digits (pixels) in the matrix.

- Padding: When a filter does not perfectly fit the input image, you can either pad the image with 0s so that the filter fits, or you can drop the part of the image where the filter does not fit.

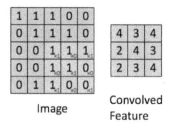

Image   Convolved Feature

Figure 7: *A single step of Convolutional Neural Network [7]*

You also need to specify the number of input channels, and the number of output channels to the model. Take the figure below, and try to guess the filter size and stride.

The image of size 5 × 5 has a filter of size 3 × 3, and a stride of 1. If you look closely in the golden matrix in the figure above, you see that the filter is not just 1s, it is a matrix of 1s and 0s. This is a specific type of filter, and the type of filter you use will help you perform different operations, like edge detection, blurring of images, sharpening images, etc. The figure below shows the various convolution images after applying different types of filters:

Operation	Filter	Convolved Image
Identity	$\begin{bmatrix} 0 & 0 & 0 \\ 0 & 1 & 0 \\ 0 & 0 & 0 \end{bmatrix}$	
Edge detection	$\begin{bmatrix} 1 & 0 & -1 \\ 0 & 0 & 0 \\ -1 & 0 & 1 \end{bmatrix}$	
	$\begin{bmatrix} 0 & 1 & 0 \\ 1 & -4 & 1 \\ 0 & 1 & 0 \end{bmatrix}$	
	$\begin{bmatrix} -1 & -1 & -1 \\ -1 & 8 & -1 \\ -1 & -1 & -1 \end{bmatrix}$	
Sharpen	$\begin{bmatrix} 0 & -1 & 0 \\ -1 & 5 & -1 \\ 0 & -1 & 0 \end{bmatrix}$	
Box blur (normalized)	$\frac{1}{9}\begin{bmatrix} 1 & 1 & 1 \\ 1 & 1 & 1 \\ 1 & 1 & 1 \end{bmatrix}$	
Gaussian blur (approximation)	$\frac{1}{16}\begin{bmatrix} 1 & 2 & 1 \\ 2 & 4 & 2 \\ 1 & 2 & 1 \end{bmatrix}$	

Figure 8: *The Effect of Filter on Images [6]*

It is possible to add an activation function to the output of the convolutional layer. The ReLU activation function performs the best in this case because it adds non-linearity in the model as a whole.

Pooling Layer

The pooling layer performs a dimensionality reduction and ultimately reduces the computational cost. It also has a positive side-effect of extracting dominant features which are rotational and positionally invariant.

This layer is very easy to understand. You will give it a 1-dimensional, 2-dimensional, or 3-dimensional matrix along with a kernel size, and it will use the kernel sized window to give the maximum number from the window as the output. If you are confused, you should look at the figure below:

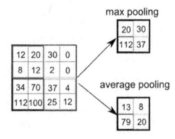

Figure 9: *Max Pooling and Average Pooling [8]*

In the figure above, the kernel size used is 2 × 2. You can understand max pooling as getting the most outstanding vector to represent the area of an image.

There are many different types of pooling like min pooling, max pooling, and average pooling. Out of all of these, max pooling works the best.

Fully Connected Layer

The last layer in the convolutional model is the fully connected layer. This layer is added to learn the non-linear combinations of the high-level features as represented by the output of the convolutional layer.

After *n* number of convolutional layers and pooling layers, the output needs to be flattened and passed to a fully connected layer. The fully connected layer is a normal feed-forward neural network. This network also needs an activation function depending on the type of model you are trying to create.

8.2.4 Transfer Learning

If you do not want to build your own CNN model, there are many CNN models available for you to use. Some of them are listed below:

- LeNet
- AlexNet
- VGGNet
- GoogLeNet
- ResNet
- ZFNet

8.3 SUMMARY

- Two main types of neural networks apart from the feed-forward network are the recurrent neural network, and the convolutional neural network.
- Recurrent neural networks are good at modelling sequential data, or time-series data.
- The traditional RNN is not good at modelling long sequences of tens of thousands of sequences.
- To process very long sequences, we are introduced to the long short-term memory network.
- A simplified form of the LSTM network is called the gated recurrent units (GRU).
- The traditional RNN, LSTM, and GRU are all different types of recurrent neural networks.
- Convolutional neural network was developed to make computer vision tasks simpler.

- CNN is preferred over the feed-forward network when it comes to computer vision tasks.

- One way of designing the model of CNN is to have the convolution layer, pooling layer, and the fully connected layer, in that order.

Now that you have reached the end of the chapter, I highly recommend you continue the learning path by visiting the GitHub repository for this chapter.

https://github.com/a-soundhararajan/machine-learning/tree/main/CNN-RNN

There is also a website (https://letsbecomemlengineers.com/) and a YouTube channel (https://www.youtube.com/channel/UCxxGU_Q6A-8aJlSGP19FYUA) with additional content.

CHAPTER 9

Natural Language Processing

Unstructured Text Data

Natural language processing (NLP) is the art of extracting information from unstructured text. A computer system only understands the language of 0s and 1s, it does not understand human languages like English or Spanish. Language as a structured medium of communication is what separates us human beings from animals. We are surrounded by written text data all the time in the form of books, emails, blogs, social media posts, news and more.

NLP is a field in machine learning which aims to help a computer understand, analyze, manipulate, and potentially generate human language. NLP is not the same as speech recognition. Text processing is the focus of NLP not speech / voice.

NLP is making huge leaps in solving industry problems in the current years, and the value of the NLP sector is estimated to be worth about 35 billion USD by 2026 based on a market research report published by MarketsandMarkets.com.

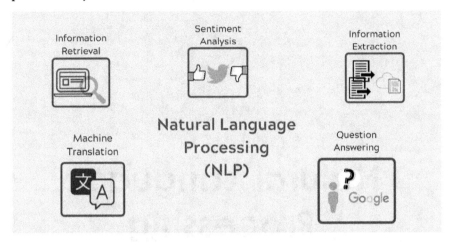

Figure 1: *Natural Language Processing [1]*

9.1 NATURAL LANGUAGE PROCESSING IN REAL LIFE

Various companies like Google, Facebook, and Amazon use NLP to bring better services to their customers. Some examples of companies using NLP are as follows:

- Google uses NLP to retrieve information, as well as categorize the data based on the information contained in the raw data. Various services like Google search, and Gmail make use of NLP algorithms. Google also has a translation service which can translate one language to another language based on NLP models.

- A website called Smmry provides its users with a summarized version of a text input. This is done through a sequence-to-sequence NLP model.

- Services like Grammarly takes a text input, checks if the sentences are grammatically correct, and it provides you with the correct sentence if the input is grammatically incorrect.

9.2 WHAT MAKES NATURAL LANGUAGE PROCESSING COMPLICATED?

More than the different dialects of the languages, the core difficulty is how humans use those languages in daily interactions. For instance, sarcasm used by humans is easily understood by other humans, but it is very difficult to program an algorithm to understand sarcasm.

On top of that, a total of 7,151 spoken languages have been classified by Ethnologue as of May 2022. Coming up with an algorithm which applies to all the languages in this world might as well be impossible. All these languages are very different from one another, take for example, how languages are written. Some are written left to right (like English), while others are written right to left (Arabic), some are written from top to bottom (Mongolian, certain Japanese dialects)! Hebrew and Arabic languages also have optional vowels.

In this book, we will only look into the English language and how to create algorithms for it. This makes the magnitude of the task smaller, but English also has its own caveats. English is word order dependent, take for example the following sentences:

Anna painted the house.

The house was painted by Anna.

Both the sentences have the same meaning, but programming that into an algorithm is more difficult than it initially appears to be.

English also has tenses which changes the spellings of the words (verbs) used as well as the meaning of the sentences completely. The tenses of English are:

Simple Past: I read the book.

Past Continuous: I was reading this book last night.

Past Perfect: I had read many books by the time I was 10.

Past Perfect Continuous: I had been reading this book for a month before you.

Simple Present: I read every day.

Present Continuous: I am reading this book.
Present Perfect: I have read so many books.
Present Perfect Continuous: I have been reading since last year.
Simple Future: I will read as much as I can next year.
Future Continuous: I will be reading War and Peace soon.
Future Perfect: I will have read this book by the end of the month.
Future Perfect Continuous: I will have been reading for an hour by 4:00 PM.

Looking at the above examples, each sentence has a different meaning even though only the tense changed.

These are some difficulties that you will face when you start with NLP tasks.

9.3 APPLICATIONS OF NATURAL LANGUAGE PROCESSING

Let's start with Google search, it uses many NLP methods to recognize what you searched for and gives you ranked search results which are relevant to you. Amazon does a similar thing when you search for products on its website. All these companies including Apple, Meta, Microsoft, and Twitter have natural language processing research groups churning out studies and achieving breakthroughs in language understanding and generation.

You certainly do not have to be a billion-dollar corporation to create meaningful NLP models. The basics of NLP is same for everyone, and you can create a lot of interesting projects, which include but are not limited to:

Text Classification
Question Answering Models
Machine Translation
Text Summarization
Reading Comprehension

These are all very fascinating projects that you can build at home, and we will look into many of them in this chapter.

The first question that we need to answer is this: how is text data stored so that we can start applying machine learning algorithms to it?

9.4 HOW IS TEXT DATA STORED?

9.4.1 Structured vs. Unstructured data:

Structured data is well organized, and it has a fixed dimension in a tabular format. It is highly specific and is stored in a predefined format.

E.g.: Employee data.

Unstructured data has no structure, no fixed dimensions - audios, videos, images, and text.

E.g.: News articles, social media posts, set of dog pictures, traffic videos.

We call a collection of text data a corpus. It can be a group of any type of text data, like news articles, collections of Tweets, books, etc.

Text data is the focus of NLP. It is the written form of a language with grammar and defined structures. Often, we also come across applied NLP which is nothing but NLP with human interaction in action.

9.4.2 How Do We Get Text Data?

You can get text data from various sources, and the easiest way is to get it online.

The first way is to scrape the data online. The internet is filled with websites with a lot of written data ready to be scrapped. You can write a web scraper program and scrape websites like Twitter, websites with forums like Reddit, Google searches, etc.

The second way is to download datasets which have already been collected for you. You can find a lot of datasets like the Amazon

Product Dataset, Stanford Question Answering Dataset (SQuAD), Yelp Reviews, and a lot more. A helpful website is Kaggle which has most of the datasets that you are looking for.

9.4.3 What Do I Do with All the Data?

With all the data that you have access to now, you either use classification or regression algorithms. Classification is usually used if you have text data because tasks like sentiment analysis (classifying emotions in text), and e-mail spam detector (classifying spam or not-spam) are classification tasks.

9.4.4 Tools for Natural Language Processing

There are a lot of Python libraries made specifically for NLP, some of the libraries are listed below:

- Natural Language Toolkit (NLTK): Natural Language Toolkit is a Python library which will let you interface with over 50 corpora and lexical resources. It also comes with a lot of functions which lets you easily classify, tokenize, stem, tag, and parse the text inputs.

- Gensim: Gensim is an open-source Python library for representing documents as semantic vectors. It is designed to process raw, unstructured digital texts using unsupervised machine learning algorithms.

Gensim has a lot of prebuilt unsupervised algorithms, such as Word2Vec, FastText, Latent Semantic Indexing (LSI, LSA), Latent Dirichlet Allocation (LDA), etc. These algorithms automatically unearth the semantic structure of documents by examining statistical co-occurrence patterns within the corpus of training documents. Once this is done, any plain text document can be expressed in new, semantic representation.

- Keras: Keras is a Python package which comes with TensorFlow. It also has some text preprocessing functions. It has a tokenizer class which can convert a text corpus into either a sequence of integers or into a vector where the coefficient for each token could be binary, based on word count, based on TF-IDF, and so on.

9.5 FEATURE EXTRACTION

Now that we have the text data, and a suite of Python Libraries, we need to convert the text into a numerical form as machine learning algorithms understand the data or features only in a numerical form.

Converting the text into a numerical form is called vectorization. Each word is represented as a vector, and a feature. Hence, you need to process every word. This applies to Twitter, product reviews / documents / book (e.g., 100,000 words = 100k features)

e.g.: Tweet : 1 sentence = 20 words = 20 vectors = 20 features

But not all features are created equal; some features will give you a better performance than others. Sometimes texts can have specific words which will change the meaning of a sentence completely if you delete them, or sometimes it does not matter if a particular word is dropped from a sentence.

Before you vectorize every word and convert it into a number for the computer to understand, you need to process the text data to make it easier for the algorithm to process and make predictions for the given problem. This processing of the data before vectorizing it is called pre-processing. Pre-processing methods are independent of text encoding techniques.

9.5.1 Pre-Processing the Data

There are a lot of ways to pre-process the data, and some of them are discussed in this section.

Lower-casing the Texts

This is used to lowercase the whole corpus so that everything is in a uniform form. It will also be helpful to reduce the unique words in the corpus because now the same words which were in different cases earlier look the same to the computer.

Tokenizing

Tokenizing is a process of splitting text content into smaller units of words/tokens. A token is a small unit of text, it can be words, phrases, characters, n-grams.

Corpus -> Documents -> Paragraphs -> Sentences -> Tokens

Now, what are those n-grams mentioned previously? Well, it is nothing but a group of 'n' number of words made into one token.

For example,
Sentence: "I love to walk."
Unigrams (n=1): I, love, to, walk
Bigrams (n=2): I love, to walk
Trigrams (n=3): I love to, love to walk

The most widely used tokenization process is the whitespace tokenizer / unigram tokenizer which is to split the text by whitespace. Another tokenizer is the regular expression tokenizer which splits the text by pattern. Tokenization can be performed at the sentence/words/character level.

Python libraries such as NLTK, Keras, and Gensim can perform tokenization for us.

Removing Unnecessary Features

You can remove unnecessary characters or words from a text if it improves the performance of the algorithm.

Stop Words: They are common words that will likely appear in any text. They do not tell us much about our data, so it is sometimes better to remove them.

Mis-spelt Words: In some texts, especially the ones written by human beings, have spelling errors in them. So, it is possible to either remove the incorrect words completely or use the NLTK package to correct the spelling of the words.

Numbers: Sometimes it is beneficial to remove the numbers completely or change them into texts. E.g., 1 -> one; 2 -> two.

Normalization

Normalization is the process of converting a token to its base form (called morpheme). It is used to reduce the data dimensionality. It removes variation in data, redundant data and keeps only the unique words.

The structure of a token will be in the form of: <prefix> <morpheme> <suffix>

E.g.: antinationalist => anti + national + ist (national is the morpheme, base form)

Two popular methods of normalization are stemming, and lemmatization.

Stemming is an elementary rule-based process of removing the inflectional forms from a token.

E.g.: laughing, laughed, laughs, laugh ==>" "la"gh"

Generally, stemming is not a good normalization technique as it produces non-meaningful terms in certain scenarios. It may give you words which are not in the dictionary.

E.g.: his teams are not winning "> "hi team are not "in"

Lemmatization is a systematic step-by-step process, it makes use of vocabulary, word structure, part-of-speech tags and grammar relations.

e.g.: running, ran, run, rans -> run
    am, is, are -> be

Part of Speech (PoS) Tagging and Grammar Tagging

Part of Speech tagging and grammar tagging use the syntax and structure related properties of a text object. The part of speech defines the usage and syntactic context of a text object. In a sentence, every word will be associated with a proper part of speech. Most commonly used parts of speech tags are provided by the Penn Treebank corpus.

The 8 parts of speech are noun, pronoun, adverb, adjective, preposition, verb, conjunction, and interjection.

E.g.: David has purchased a new laptop from the Apple Store.

David, laptop, Apple Store – subjec"; "has purcha"ed" – verb; n–w - adjective

Parts of speech are primarily used in text cleaning, feature engineering tasks, word sense disambiguation.

E.g.: Please book a flight to New York vs. I like to read a book in New York (The meaning of the word "book" differs based on context).

Once the pre-processing steps are complete, we move on to vectorizing the data.

9.5.2 Vectorizing the Data

Vectorization is the process of converting text into arrays of numbers for the computer to process. There are many ways to do this, but people are increasingly using Word Embeddings to vectorize the data. We will look at some of the methods below:

Bag-of-Words

A bag-of-words, much like the name, is like a bag where all the words of a corpus are stored. It involves the whole vocabulary of all the words in the corpus.

It is called 'bag' because any information about the order or structure of the words in the input is discarded. This bag-of-words model only cares if the word occurs in the document, not where in the document.

TF-IDF

It stands for Term Frequency-Inverse Document Frequency. This is meant to show how important a word is in the context of the whole document.

The first part of TF-IDF, which is the TF (Term Frequency), is shown by the formula below:

$$tf(t, d) = 0.5 + 0.5 \cdot \frac{f_{t,d}}{\sum_{t' \in d} f_{t',d}}$$

where $f_{t,d}$ is the number of times a term t occurs in a document d. The denominator is the total number of terms in the document d.

The second part of TF-IDF, which is IDF (Inverse Document Frequency) is shown by the formula below:

$$idf(t, D) = \log \frac{N}{1 + |\{d \in D : t \in d\}|}$$

where, N is the total number of documents in the corpus, is the number of documents where the term t appears. 1 is added to the formula because you do not want to divide with 0 when a term does not exist in the document.

Finally, TF-IDF is calculated by:

$$tfidf(t, d, D) = tf(t, d) \times idf(t, D)$$

Theoretically, TF-IDF should balance the words which appear too frequently in a corpus and the words which appear less frequently but is relatively more important to the overall meaning of the whole document.

Word2Vec

Word2vec is not a singular algorithm, but it is a family of model architectures and optimizations that can be used to learn word embeddings from large datasets.

Deep Learning Trained Word Embeddings

- GPT-3: It is a pre-trained model by OpenAI. This model has been trained on 175 billion parameters.

- BERT: Google's Bidirectional Encoder Representations from Transformers (BERT) has been trained on 2,500 million words from Wikipedia and 800 million words from Book Corpus.

- RoBERTa: Facebook's RoBERTa is a transformers model pre-trained on a large corpus of data in a self-supervised fashion (meaning it was trained pre-trained on the raw texts only, without humans labelling them in any way). RoBERTa has also been trained on more data than BERT for an extended amount of time.

9.6 MACHINE LEARNING ALGORITHMS

In this section of the chapter, let's look at some applications of machine learning algorithms and understand a bit about how they are applied in NLP problems.

9.6.1 Classification

When it comes to natural language processing, classification tasks include sentiment analysis, e-mail spam detection, language detection, topic labelling, etc.

Classification can be performed with machine learning algorithms such as support vector machines, and naïve Bayes algorithms.

Support Vector Machines: It is a machine learning algorithm which tries to find a decision boundary that optimally separates the classified data points. The distance from the decision surface to the closest data point determines the margin of the classifier. The decision boundary can classify different points of text data, so it can be used for text data.

Naïve Bayes Algorithms: This is a group of algorithms which apply the Bayes theorem. The only thing to consider when applying this theorem is that every feature should be independent of each other. These algorithms are used in NLP to predict tags of the text content, and the probability of a certain tag from many tags.

9.6.2 Clustering

Clustering is used to group similar data points together. In terms of text corpus, it can cluster similar words together. Algorithms like the k-means algorithms are used to cluster data points.

k-means algorithms are unsupervised, and you need to define the number of clusters that you want from the data. Sometimes the number of clusters are apparent (for example, sentiment analysis will have 2 or 5 clusters depending on the output you want), but at other times you will have to apply more complicated methods of defining the number of clusters.

9.6.3 Tagging

Tagging for natural language processing includes parts of speech tagging, grammar tagging and a lot more. You can create a decision trees algorithm, or a random forest algorithm to tag the words of natural languages.

9.6.4 Word Vectors

Word vectors are specific matrix of numbers of each word in a language or a subset of language. These are very effective and can improve the performance of algorithms. There are a lot of vectors which have already been trained on a large corpus of data, like Word2Vec, and GloVe. But you can create your own word vectors by using an algorithm called principal component analysis (PCA).

To do this, you need to create a word correspondence matrix and apply the PCA over that matrix to get the word embeddings. There is a research paper titled "Word Embeddings through Hellinger PCA" which used the Hellinger distance to create a word2word correspondence matrix. Then they applied PCA over that matrix to get the word embeddings in the number of dimensions that were needed. This paper showed that the PCA method is comparable to GloVe and Word2Vec.

9.7 DEEP LEARNING

Neural networks are much better compared to other machine learning algorithms if there is a lot of data to be fed into the model. If you have more data, then it is highly recommended to use neural networks since it performs better almost every time.

9.7.1 Classification Tasks

RNN's LSTM and GRU perform similarly in natural language tasks but there is one thing which sets them apart. If you have a smaller dataset then it is better to use GRU as opposed to LSTM because it has been discovered that GRUs train faster and perform better than LSTMs on less training data for language modeling tasks.

9.7.2 Sequence-to-Sequence Models

Sequence-to-sequence models are a specific type of architecture which are used to create models that take in a length of text (sequence of text) and output a sequence of text. There are many products which use these models, like Chatbots, Machine Translation, etc.

Encoder-Decoder Models

These models have an encoder and a decoder with an encoder vector connecting the two together.

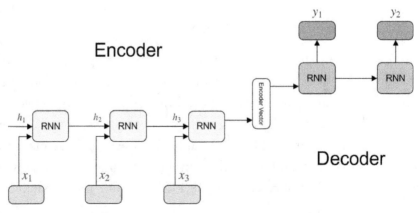

Figure 2: *The Encoder-Decoder Model [2]*

The figure above shows the encoder-decoder model. We will look at each part of the model in more detail here:

Encoder: The encoder is a stack of recurrent units (LSTMs, GRUs, RNNs), where each unit accepts a single input element. Each unit collects information from that part of the sequence and passes it forward.

For example, the input can be a sentence which you want to translate into another language.

Encoder Vector: The encoder vector is the final hidden state in the encoder section of the model. This final hidden state will have a condensed version of the input data containing all the most important parts that are helpful for the model to reduce error.

Decoder: This is also a stack of recurrent units, where each unit predicts an output at a time step *t*.

9.7.3 Transformers

This is arguably the most important model in NLP, even the billions of Google searches done every day uses BERT which is a variation of this model. This model was introduced in 2017 by a team at Google Brain in the paper that is aptly titled "Attention Is All You Need". Transformers are a sequence-to-sequence neural network similar to the one described above but without recurrent units.

One thing that set the transformers apart from other models is their attention mechanism. Much like the attention of human beings, attention in transformers looks at an input sequence and decides at each step which parts of the sequence are important.

For example, when you provide an input to a transformer, it might keep in its memory all the most important and relevant keywords from the input.

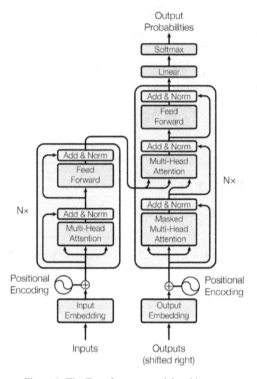

Figure 1: The Transformer - model architecture.

Figure 3: *The Transformer - Model Architecture [3]*

The figure above shows the transformer model. We will not go into the details of this model because it is beyond the scope of this book, but if you want to do any substantial work in the field of NLP then it is highly recommended that you learn about transformers, and read the paper titled "Attention Is All You Need".

9.8 SUMMARY

- Natural Language Processing (NLP) is a way to make sense of unstructured text data.

- NLP is hard due to the fact that there are thousands of human languages with their own rules of communication.

- NLP data can be easily scrapped from online sources, or you can download pre-processed data from websites like Kaggle.

- There are a lot of libraries like NLTK, and Gensim that makes your life a lot easier when processing these datasets.
- You should first pre-process your text data by lowercasing everything, removing stop words, and stemming or lemmatizing it.
- After pre-processing your data, you should convert those texts into vectors. The best way to vectorize your data is using word embedding techniques. Alternatively, you can also train your own embedding layer if you are doing a deep learning project.
- Depending on whether you want to classify, cluster, tag or create word vectors, there are specific machine learning algorithms that you should investigate for each purpose.
- Deep learning models work better than machine learning models if you have more data.
- Recurrent neural networks like LSTM and GRU are the best basic building blocks when it comes to NLP due to them having memory and performing exceptionally for time-series data.
- Transformers and their variations like BERT are currently the state-of-the-art models when performing NLP tasks.

Now that you have reached the end of the chapter, I highly recommend you continue the learning path by visiting the GitHub repository for this chapter.

https://github.com/a-soundhararajan/machine-learning/tree/main/NLP

There is also a website (https://letsbecomemlengineers.com/) and a YouTube channel (https://www.youtube.com/channel/UCxxGU_Q6A-8aJlSGP19FYUA) with additional content.

CHAPTER 10

The Machine Learning Engineer

Next Steps

Looks like you have made it to the end of the book. Are you a software engineer who is looking for the next challenge or someone wishing to replace their age-old skills like COBOL/ Mainframe with machine learning? Are you someone who likes having an advantage over other candidates in the job market? Or someone who enjoys research and learning something new every single day? If your answer is a yes to any of those questions, then you need to start investing your time in machine learning immediately.

Do I need to have a computer science background or a data science background?

Absolutely NOT. Machine learning is a wide field with plenty of opportunities for people who do not come from a software background. Domain experts devote time to the data annotation section of supervised learning.

Do I need to have programming experience?

No, but you do need to have strong analytical skills and an engineering mindset to understand the relationship within the data, and you should be willing to identify patterns in the data.

Data engineers prepare the data to train the machine learning model and setup the data pipelines for data scientists and machine learning engineers to explore the data and build a model.

Do I have to develop new machine learning algorithms from scratch?

This depends on your interests, you can if you want to. But a general machine learning engineer does not have to develop machine learning algorithms from scratch. Even data scientists have no day-to-day need to develop machine learning algorithms. Academic experts have already developed plenty of them to solve real-time problems. If you have 2–3-years of programming experience, and you know Python, then you are ready to use the tons of machine learning libraries available for free.

10.1 MATHEMATICS

You might be thinking to yourself, but mathematics is not my favorite subject. Even if math is not your favorite subject, if you are not completely disgusted by it, then you are fine. You just need enough math to understand the data patterns, and to explore the data.

If you dislike math, you can focus mostly on writing the code to develop machine learning models or designing the runtime infrastructure for the machine learning pipeline. You can work with data scientists when you have a need to do deep dive on the data.

Becoming a data engineer is a great option if you are not a big fan of math and do not like reading research papers with too many formulas.

If you absolutely love mathematics, then you can become either a data scientist or a machine learning engineer that understands the data and creates focused solutions for every problem that you face. When it comes to machine learning, the most important thing is that you are willing to learn and keep on learning every single day. It is a field that is growing at a rapid speed, it will take at least 5-10 years to reach maturity. To be at the cutting-edge of machine learning, you need to keep up-to-date on the recent developments takes place on a regular basis. The difference between machine learning and the traditional software development is that, in machine learning, it is expected that you learn continuously.

10.2 MACHINE LEARNING ENGINEER VS. DATA SCIENTIST

A machine learning engineer works closely with data scientists and data engineers on a regular basis.

The process begins with the data scientist. A data scientist performs the data exploration, feature selections and comes up with the initial model to solve the problem as a proof of concept. Then a machine learning engineer will take the initial model to validate it against business objectives, optimize the model and take it through the training process. Once the model performs at a satisfactory prediction rate, the ML engineer designs model runtime machine pipeline infrastructure, and deploys the model in the form an API (most likely) for real-time prediction of the customer traffic. The machine learning engineer also ensures the reliability aspects of ML pipeline systems – DevOps, scaling and monitoring.

10.3 MACHINE LEARNING ENGINEER VS. TRADITIONAL SOFTWARE ENGINEER

As a software engineer, you will have more clarity on the day-to-day tasks. But a machine learning engineer has ambiguity and more of a trial-and-error process. There are no definitive, clear-cut and guaranteed outcomes. A machine learning model is often a black box that spits out predictions and you do not know why you get this outcome vs. that for a few scenarios.

The most significant difference between a software engineer's and an ML engineer's day-to-day life is the "iteration time". A software engineer can change a few lines of code and rerun it to see if it works. On the other hand, when a machine learning engineer changes a small thing in any of the steps, he must wait minutes, hours, or days to see if that change made any difference or not. On a normal day, a machine learning engineer might spend time on data annotation, modeling, training, or supporting the inference infrastructure.

10.4 RESPONSIBILITIES OF A MACHINE LEARNING ENGINEER

Here are some responsibilities that a machine learning engineer has:
- Analyzing machine learning algorithms to solve a given problem.
- Exploring and visualizing the data.
- Identifying the differences in data distribution.
- Verifying data quality and ensuring the data quality through data cleaning.
- Defining validation strategies.
- Understanding the business objectives and developing models.
- Managing machine learning model infrastructure and the pipeline.

10.5 JOB OPPORTUNITIES FOR MACHINE LEARNING ENGINEERS

Until 2015, the majority of machine learning opportunities were mainly from top innovative companies like Apple, Amazon, Meta (Facebook), Google, and Twitter. Now machine learning has expanded to the next set of IT driven companies like Uber, Airbnb, and more. Core sectors like finance, healthcare, and retail companies have started investing in their data division and adapting to leverage machine learning models to elevate their business and stay competitive in the market.

Most mid-sized companies are still in the discovery phase and are trying to understand how they can leverage machine learning capabilities to serve their customers better. The demand for machine learning engineers is steadily increasing, and it is estimated that it will hit peak state in 2025. You should not wait any longer to wet your hands in the machine learning ocean. The industry is just starting to scratch the surface of the capabilities of machine learning, and machine learning has so much more to offer.

Based on an Indeed report published in 2021, machine learning job openings are on the top in all aspects (including salary, number of postings, and industry demand). Between 2015-2018, machine learning job postings have increased by 344% and the base compensation hit $146,085.

If you are excited about massive data, automation, and algorithms, machine learning is the correct place for you to move to. No two days will ever be the same, you will always be doing something different every single day.

Machine learning has so many career paths you could choose from. There are many engineers who are specialized in one particular area of machine learning. You could specialize in natural language and create NLP models, or you could specialize in computer vision, object localization and detection, amongst many other areas of interest.

In all different areas of expertise, you can choose to be a machine learning engineer, a data scientist, or a data engineer. There is a high demand but a low supply for people with machine learning skills.

10.6 WHAT IS THE NEXT STEP?

Learning the fundamentals is one thing, the next important thing is to start applying what you have learnt. It is all about taking the first baby steps, you should spend at least 15-30 minutes every day on Jupyter notebooks to get yourself familiar with the Python Sci-kit Learn Library. There are tons of readily available datasets on www.kaggle.com to develop basic models and get comfortable with the training process and model evaluation metrics.

TensorFlow playground is another great place to spend time designing your neural networks and get a taste 'of the forward and backward propagation process and understand the impact of various activation functions.

10.7 HOW CAN I ESTABLISH CREDIBILITY AS A MACHINE LEARNING ENGINEER?

Once you are solid on the fundamentals, start participating in Kaggle competitions or volunteer for research projects on www.omdena.com. You can also start your machine learning pet projects and have your notebook files in git. You can add your Git repository to your resume and LinkedIn profile to show your hands-on experience. Top companies clearly understand that bringing real-world industry experience to the job is hard as most of the companies are still in discovery phase.

Machine learning cloud certifications are another great way to showcase your expertise. These certifications will empower you with the knowledge you need to build a machine learning pipeline for a given problem. Here are some certifications you can get:
- AWS Certified Machine Learning – Specialty
- Microsoft Certified Azure Data Scientist Associate
- Professional Machine Learning Engineer by Google

There are also 10-to-12-week crash courses or bootcamp sessions from top universities.
- Machine Learning Certificate Course by Andrew NG, Stanford
- Machine Learning & Artificial Intelligence Certificate course by MIT

- Machine Learning Certificate Course by Harvard

10.8 SUMMARY

- If you are interested in pursuing your goal of becoming a machine learning engineer, you should go beyond exploring this book.

- You do not need a computer science background, nor do you need a degree in mathematics to become a machine learning engineer.

- The main characteristic of a machine learning engineer is to have a life-long love for learning new things because there will always be something to learn in the field of machine learning.

- Machine learning engineering is different from traditional software engineering because machine learning engineers cannot produce definitive clear-cut outcomes. They spend most of their time in analysis and tuning model behavior by adjusting various parameters.

- Since machine learning is still a young field, there are more and more companies starting to hire machine learning engineers.

- Machine learning engineers get paid 30-50% more than traditional software engineers.

- If you are interested in becoming a machine learning engineer, you should start doing projects of your own to get a solid foundation on things that are important.

- Pursuing a machine learning certification course is also a good way to get credibility as a machine learning engineer.

Happy coding and let's become machine learning engineers to transform people's lives in the data world!

As part of this book, I have created a website and a YouTube channel to take your learnings to the next level. You can head over to https://letsbecomemlengineers.com and https://www. youtube.com/ channel/UCxxGU_Q6A-8aJlSGP19FYUA to learn further.

Don't let your learning
lead to knowledge.

Let your learning lead to action.

— Jim Rohn, Motivational Speaker

References

CHAPTER 1

Hands-On Machine Learning with Scikit-Learn, Keras, and TensorFlow: Concepts, Tools, and Techniques to Build Intelligent Systems By Geron Aurelien

Machine Learning 101 - SlideShare. https://www.slideshare.net/TalhaObaid1/machine-learning-101

Artificial intelligence: the new electricity. https://www.wipo.int/wipo_magazine/en/2019/03/article_0001.html

Mark Kuban's quote on the importance of knowing Machine Learning. https://quotecatalog.com/quote/mark-cuban-artificial-inte-x1mzEG7/

Understanding the Basics of Supervised Learning and Reinforced Learning. https://www.analyticsinsight.net/understanding-basics-supervised-learning-reinforced-learning/

CHAPTER 2

[1] CrowdFlower Data science report: https://visit.figure-eight.com/rs/416-ZBE-142/images/CrowdFlower_DataScienceReport_2016.pdf.

Data Scientists Spend Most of Their Time Cleaning Data
https://whatsthebigdata.com/2016/05/01/data-scientists-spend-most-of-
their-time-cleaning-data/

How Much Data Is Created Every Day?
https://seedscientific.com/how-much-data-is-created-every-day/

Exploratory Data Analysis — an important part of any analytical
strategy! https://medium.com/quarkanalytics/exploratory-data-analysis-
an-important-part-of-any-analytical-strategy-1f7a48bb3462

Titanic - Machine Learning from Disaster
https://www.kaggle.com/c/titanic/data

Fundamental Techniques of Feature Engineering for Machine Learning
https://towardsdatascience.com/feature-engineering-for-machine-
learning-3a5e293a5114

CHAPTER 3

20 Popular Machine Learning Metrics. Part 1
https://towardsdatascience.com/20-popular-machine-learning-metrics-
part-1-classification-regression-evaluation-metrics-1ca3e282a2ce

Metrics to Evaluate your Machine Learning Algorithm
https://towardsdatascience.com/metrics-to-evaluate-your-machine-
learning-algorithm-f10ba6e38234

Evaluation Metrics Machine Learning - Analytics Vidhya https://www.
analyticsvidhya.com/blog/2019/08/11-important-model-evaluation-error-
metrics/

A Gentle Introduction to k-fold Cross-Validation.
https://machinelearningmastery.com/k-fold-cross-validation/

Top 8 Challenges for Machine Learning Practitioners
https://towardsdatascience.com/top-8-challenges-for-machine-learning-
practitioners-c4c0130701a1

5 Challenges of Machine Learning!
https://www.analyticsvidhya.com/blog/2021/06/5-challenges-of-machine-learning/

CHAPTER 4

[1] M. W. Toews, "Standard Deviation," 9 Feburary 2005. [Online]. Available: https://upload.wikimedia.org/wikipedia/commons/8/8c/Standard_deviation_diagram.svg. [Accessed 7 March 2022].

[2] CueMath, "Quartile Formula - What is Quartile Formula?," [Online]. Available: https://www.cuemath.com/quartile-formula/. [Accessed 7 March 2022].

[3] ck12, "Graphs of Linear Functions," [Online]. Available: https://www.ck12.org/c/algebra/graph-using-intercepts/lesson/Graphs-of-Linear-Functions-BSC-ALG/. [Accessed 7 March 2022].

[4] X. Lu, H. Sun, T. Niu and Z. Cao, "A Simplified Method of Radiator to Improve the Simulation Speed of Room Temperature Distribution," in *International Symposium on Simulation and Process Modelling*, 2020.

[5] Brilliant Mathematics, "Calculating Slope," [Online]. Available: https://brilliant.org/wiki/calculating-slope/. [Accessed 7 March 2022].

[6] L. Pennington, "Convex: Definition, Shape & Function," [Online]. Available: https://study.com/academy/lesson/convex-definition-shape-function.html. [Accessed 7 March 2022].

[7] B. Veytsman, "Thermodynamic Stability," 1997. [Online]. Available: https://borisv.lk.net/matsc597c-1997/introduction/Lecture5/node2.html. [Accessed 8 March 2022].

[8] E. Raza, "Gradient Descent," 5 September 2019. [Online]. Available: https://medium.com/@raza.shan83/gradient-descent-c568801d0b62. [Accessed 8 March 2022].

Mathematics Behind Machine Learning | Data Science. https://www.analyticsvidhya.com/blog/2019/10/mathematics-behind-machine-learning/

Mathematics For Machine Learning? What Concepts do You Need to master's in data science? https://www.analyticsvidhya.com/blog/2021/06/how-to-learn-mathematics-for-machine-learning-what-concepts-do-you-need-to-master-in-data-science/

A quick introduction to derivatives for machine learning people. https://towardsdatascience.com/a-quick-introduction-to-derivatives-for-machine-learning-people-3cd913c5cf33

All you need to know about Gradient Descent. https://medium.com/analytics-vidhya/all-you-need-to-know-about-gradient-descent-f0178c19131d

Gradient Descent for Machine Learning. https://machinelearningmastery.com/gradient-descent-for-machine-learning/

CHAPTER 5

[1] Sewaqu, "Linear Regression," 4 November 2010. [Online]. Available: https://simple.wikipedia.org/wiki/Linear_regression#/media/File:Linear_regression.svg. [Accessed 19 March 2022].

[2] Qef, "Logistic Curve," 1 July 2008. [Online]. Available: https://en.wikipedia.org/wiki/Logistic_function#/media/File:Logistic-curve.svg. [Accessed 19 March 2022].

[3] R. Gandhi, "Support Vector Machine — Introduction to Machine Learning Algorithms," 7 June 2018. [Online]. Available: https://towardsdatascience.com/support-vector-machine-introduction-to-machine-learning-algorithms-934a444fca47. [Accessed 19 March 2022].

[4] B. Stecanella, "Support Vector Machines (SVM) Algorithm Explained," 22 June 2017. [Online]. Available: https://monkeylearn. com/blog/introduction-to-support-vector-machines-svm/. [Accessed 19 March 2022].

[5] G. Chauhan`, "k-NN (k-Nearest Neighbors) Starter Guide," 24 February 2021. [Online]. Available: https://machinelearninghd. com/k-nn-k-nearest-neighbors-starter-guide/. [Accessed 19 March 2022].

[6] F. N. Arain, "Decision Tree Classification Algorithm," [Online]. Available: https://www.devops.ae/decision-tree-classification-algorithm/. [Accessed 19 March 2022].

[7] I. Athanasiadis, "Training Intelligent Agents in the Semantic Web Era: The Golf Advisor Agent," in *IEEE WIC ACM International Conference on Web Intelligence (WI)*, 2007.

[8] J. Le, "R Decision Trees Tutorial," 19 June 2018. [Online]. Available: https://www.datacamp.com/community/tutorials/decision-trees-R. [Accessed 19 March 2022].

Linear Regression for Machine Learning. https://machinelearningmastery.com/linear-regression-for-machine-learning

Logistic Regression - an overview | ScienceDirect Topics. https://www.sciencedirect.com/topics/computer-science/logistic-regression

Naive Bayes Classifier. What is a classifier? https://towardsdatascience.com/naive-bayes-classifier-81d512f50a7c

Support Vector Machine — Introduction to Machine Learning https://towardsdatascience.com/support-vector-machine-introduction-to-machine-learning-algorithms-934a444fca47

Machine Learning Basics with the K-Nearest Neighbors. https://towardsdatascience.com/machine-learning-basics-with-the-k-nearest-neighbors-algorithm-6a6e71d01761

K-Nearest Neighbors Algorithm in Python and Scikit-Learn.
https://stackabuse.com/k-nearest-neighbors-algorithm-in-python-and-scikit-learn/

Decision Tree Algorithm - A Complete Guide. https://www.analyticsvidhya.com/blog/2021/08/decision-tree-algorithm/

Decision Trees in Machine Learning.
https://towardsdatascience.com/decision-trees-in-machine-learning-641b9c4e8052

Understanding Random Forest.
https://towardsdatascience.com/understanding-random-forest-58381e0602d2

CHAPTER 6

[1] Data Flair, "Clustering in Machine Learning – Algorithms that Every Data Scientist Uses," [Online]. Available: https://data-flair.training/blogs/clustering-in-machine-learning/. [Accessed 19 March 2022].

[2] A. Chello, "Unsupervised Machine Learning: K-Means Clustering with Applications in Finance," 13 October 2021. [Online]. Available: https://medium.com/the-quant-journey/unsupervised-machine-learning-k-means-clustering-with-applications-in-finance-fbabd3f187f6. [Accessed 19 March 2022].

[3] A. Gupta, "Elbow Method for optimal value of k in KMeans," 9 February 2021. [Online]. Available: https://www.geeksforgeeks.org/elbow-method-for-optimal-value-of-k-in-kmeans/. [Accessed 19 March 2022].

[4] Prwatech, "Principle Component Analysis Tutorial," 27 February 2020. [Online]. Available: https://prwatech.in/blog/machine-learning/principal-component-analysis-tutorial/. [Accessed 19 March 2022].

Unsupervised Machine Learning in Azure Machine Learning Studio. https://www.pluralsight.com/guides/unsupervised-machine-learning-in-azure-machine-learning-studio

K-Means -Introduction to Unsupervised Learning. https://www.coursera.org/lecture/ibm-unsupervised-machine-learning/

The Complete Guide to Unsupervised Learning. https://towardsdatascience.com/the-complete-guide-to-unsupervised-learning-ecf8b676f2af

CHAPTER 7

[1] C. D. Costa, "What is Machine Learning & Deep Learning," 26 10 2019. [Online]. Available: https://medium.com/@harish_6956/what-is-machine-learning-deep-learning-7788604004da. [Accessed 04 03 2022].

[2] J. Brownlee, "How to Develop a GAN for Generating MNIST Handwritten Digits," 1 September 2020. [Online]. Available: https://machinelearningmastery.com/how-to-develop-a-generative-adversarial-network-for-an-mnist-handwritten-digits-from-scratch-in-keras/. [Accessed 4 March 2022].

[3] ajitjaokar, "How to learn the maths of Data Science using your high school maths knowledge," 14 June 2019. [Online]. Available: https://www.datasciencecentral.com/how-to-learn-the-maths-of-data-science-using-your-high-school/. [Accessed 4 March 2022].

[4] AI-Master, "Sigmoid Function Logistic Regression," [Online]. Available: https://ai-master.gitbooks.io/logistic-regression/content/sigmoid-function.html. [Accessed 4 March 2022].

[5] A. Prasad, "Feed Forward Neural Networks – Intuition on Forward Propagation," 25 October 2021. [Online]. Available: https://www.analyticsvidhya.com/blog/2021/10/feed-forward-neural-networks-intuition-on-forward-propagation/. [Accessed 4 March 2022].

[6] H. Samson, "Getting to know Activation Functions in Neural Networks.," 25 June 2020. [Online]. Available: https://towardsdatascience.com/getting-to-know-activation-functions-in-neural-networks-125405b67428. [Accessed 4 March 2022].

[7] N. Ching, "Linear Regression using NumPy," 18 June 2020. [Online]. Available: https://git hub.com/nolll77/Linear-Regression-using-numpy.polyfit. [Accessed 4 March 2022].

[8] Tutorial Example, "Understand tanh(x) Activation Function: Why You Use it in Neural Networks," 17 October 2020. [Online]. Available: https://www.tutorialexample.com/understand-tanhx-activation-function-why-you-use-it-in-neural-networks. [Accessed 4 March 2022].

[9] J. Brownlee, "A Gentle Introduction to the Rectified Linear Unit (ReLU)," 9 January 2019. [Online]. Available: https://machinelearningmastery.com/rectified-linear-activation-function-for-deep-learning-neural-networks. [Accessed 4 March 2022].

[10] S. Singh, "Leaky ReLU as an Activation Function in Neural Networks," [Online]. Available: https://deeplearninguniversity.com/leaky-relu-as-an-activation-function-in-neural-networks. [Accessed 4 March 2022].

[11] A. Amini, "Non-convex optimization. We utilize stochastic gradient descent to find a local optimum in our loss landscape.," May 2018. [Online]. Available: https://www.researchgate.net/figure/Non-convex-optimization-We-utilize-stochastic-gradient-descent-to-find-a-local-optimum_fig1_325142728. [Accessed 4 March 2022].

[12] Genesis, "Gradient Descent- Part 2," 16 June 2018. [Online]. Available: https://www.fromthegenesis.com/gradient-descent-part-2/. [Accessed 4 March 2022].

Neural networks and deep learning.
http://neuralnetworksanddeeplearning.com

Recognizing handwritten digits using neural networks. https://blockgeni.com/recognizing-handwritten-digits-using-neural-networks

Deep Learning For Dummies by John Mueller and Luca Massaron

CHAPTER 8

[1] Ixnay, "File:Recurrent neural network unfold.svg," 19 June 2017. [Online]. Available: https://en.wikipedia.org/wiki/File:Recurrent_ neural_network_unfold.svg. [Accessed 4 March 2022].

[2] Colah, "Understanding LSTM Networks," 27 August 2015. [Online]. Available: https://colah.github.io/posts/2015-08-Understanding-LSTMs. [Accessed 4 March 2022].

[3] Y. Li, "Stock Price Specific LSTM," 5 December 2019. [Online]. Available: https://github.com/MRYingLEE/Stock-Price-Specific-LSTM. [Accessed 4 March 2022].

[4] dProgrammer, "RNN, LSTM & GRU," [Online]. Available: http:// dprogrammer.org/rnn-lstm-gru. [Accessed 4 March 2022].

[5] A. H. Reynolds, "Convolutional Neural Networks (CNNs)," 2019. [Online]. Available: https://anhreynolds.com/blogs/cnn.html. [Accessed 4 March 2022].

[6] Mhossain, "Easy way to understand Convolutional Neural Network: It's Easy!!!," 19 April 2019. [Online]. Available: https://medium.com/@_moazzemhossain/easy-way-to-understand-convolutional-neural-network-its-easy-d9b7c0c5adb3. [Accessed 4 March 2022].

[7] S. Rekha, "1: 5X5 input image and 3X3 Filter.," March 2018. [Online]. Available: https://www.researchgate.net/figure/5X5-input-image-and-3X3-Filter-Source-11-After-each-convolution-operation-a_fig1_324219387. [Accessed 4 March 2022].

[8] P. Mahajan, "Max Pooling," 5 July 2020. [Online]. Available: https://poojamahajan5131.medium.com/max-pooling-210fc94c4f11. [Accessed 4 March 2022].

A Comprehensive Guide to Convolutional Neural Networks. https://towardsdatascience.com/a-comprehensive-guide-to-convolutional-neural-networks-the-eli5-way-3bd2b1164a53

CNN for Deep Learning | Convolutional Neural Networks. https://www.analyticsvidhya.com/blog/2021/05/convolutional-neural-networks-cnn/

What are convolutional neural networks (CNN)? - TechTalks. https://bdtechtalks.com/2020/01/06/convolutional-neural-networks-cnn-convnets/

An Introduction to Recurrent Neural Networks. https://machinelearningmastery.com/an-introduction-to-recurrent-neural-networks-and-the-math-that-powers-them/

CHAPTER 9

[1] C. Solitaire, "natural-language-processing-exercises," 19 November 2020. [Online]. Available: https://github.com/CSolitaire/natural-language-processing-exercises. [Accessed 17 March 2022].

[2] S. Kostadinov, "Understanding Encoder-Decoder Sequence to Sequence Model," 5 February 2019. [Online]. Available: https://towardsdatascience.com/understanding-encoder-decoder-sequence-to-sequence-model-679e04af4346. [Accessed 17 March 2022].

[3] A. Vaswani, N. Shazeer, N. Parmar, J. Uszkoreit, L. Jones, A. N. Gomez, L. Kaiser and I. Polosukhin, "Attention is All You Need," in *31st Conference on Neural Information Processing Systems (NIPS 2017)*, Long Beach, 2017.

Introduction to NLP.
https://courses.analyticsvidhya.com/courses/Intro-to-NLP

Natural Language Processing (NLP) for Machine Learning. https://towardsdatascience.com/natural-language-processing-nlp-for-machine-learning-d44498845d5b.

Natural Language Processing using NLTK and Wordnet (1). http://ijcsit.com/docs/Volume%206/vol6issue06/ijcsit20150606134.pdf

Top 8 Pre-Trained NLP Models Developers Must Know. https://analyticsindiamag.com/top-8-pre-trained-nlp-models-developers-must-know/

NLP Market Research
https://www.marketsandmarkets.com/Market-Reports/natural-language-processing-nlp-825.html

CHAPTER 10

Is Machine Learning a Good Career?
https://brainstation.io/career-guides/is-machine-learning-a-good-career
Hype around Machine Learning.
https://medium.com/analytics-vidhya/hype-around-machine-learning-1a80283d7655

About the Author

Ananda Soundhararajan believes in continuous learning and lives by the principle that every single day counts. An engineering leader who has been developing and delivering software for about two decades. Expert in APIs and specialized in API Gateway technologies, and a big advocate of Cloud and DevOps transformation. He has published a white paper on non-relational database systems at Compuware Corporation in 2011. Ananda  holds a Bachelor of Engineering in Computer Science from SSN College of Engineering, Anna University, Chennai, India.

An active marathon runner, and promotes physical and mental health as the number.1 priority.

Toastmaster since 2018 and holds an officer role (VP of Public Relations) at Lake County Toastmasters.

Volunteer of Girl Scouts of Greater Chicago and Northwest Indiana.

Ananda spends his free time with family, gardening, and walking through nature trails.

To learn more about the author, visit https://www.linkedin.com/in/ananda-soundhararajan

YouTube channel: https://www.youtube.com/channel/UCxxGU_Q6A-8aJlSGP19FYUA

Don't forget to visit www.lakecountytoastmasters.com if you have the appetite to work on your public speaking and leadership skills.

Thank You for Reading My Book!

Don't forget to leave a review!

I really appreciate all of your feedback and

I would love to hear what you have to say.

Head over to Amazon or wherever you purchased this book to leave an honest review for me.

www.letsbecomemlengineers.com review

Thank you so much!

– **Ananda Soundhararajan**

www.ingramcontent.com/pod-product-compliance
Lightning Source LLC
LaVergne TN
LVHW051232050326
832903LV00028B/2369